Struck by Living

From Depression to Hope

Julie K. Hersh

Brown Books Publishing Group
Dallas, Texas

Struck by Living:
From Depression to Hope

© 2010 Julie Hersh

Manufactured in the United States of America.

For information please contact:
Brown Books Publishing Group
16200 North Dallas Parkway, Suite 170
Dallas, Texas 75248
www.brownbooks.com
972-381-0009

A New Era in Publishing™

ISBN-13: 978-1-934812-63-1
ISBN-10: 1-934812-63-3

LCCN: 2010920708
1 2 3 4 5 6 7 8 9 10

This book is intended to reflect the life experiences of the author and in no
way should it be considered to be medical advice, recommendations for
treatment, or a replacement for medical care given by physicians or trained
medical personnel.

For all those who have contemplated suicide
or succumbed to the idea, as well as the family, friends,
counselors, and medical professionals who have helped
convince us that life is worth living. I hope my
story gives you hope.

Self-deceit is a strong fort;

It will last a lifetime.

Self-truth is a lightning bolt lost as I grasp it.

And the fires that it strikes can raze my house.

You ask me to yearn after truth, Lord,

But who would choose to be whipped with fire?

Unless in the burning there can be great light,

Unless the lightning that strikes terror

Lights enough to show the boundaries

Where terror ends,

And at the limits, still enduring and alive,

Shows me myself

And a hope no longer blind.

Joanne Greenberg

Contents

I

The Garage

I tried to kill myself three times.

The third time had to work. My SUV idled with promise. I closed my eyes and tried to relax.

Guitar strums filled my finely upholstered inner sanctuary. My break-of-day mission kept the music at a distance. I couldn't feel the notes. The sound no longer rumbled in my chest.

My fingers brushed against smooth bucket seats while my nose twitched, filled with the scent of untainted leather. The Escalade ran in park, the garage door closed. My map showed a permanent destination.

I leaned forward to advance the CD, and my seatbelt pulled. "Idiot." I unbuckled the belt. No policeman patrolled my garage. No need for a safety harness; I wanted to end my life. I wanted death with no blood, fast and certain.

Before this third try, I ticked through options on my back porch. No guns or knives—too messy, painful. Pills seemed risky, a noose grueling. I weighed alternatives with precision, a chart forming in my mind. Each plus and minus lined up with cold logic.

Five months earlier, on the first attempt, I scratched a note and held a knife but could not cut. My husband, Ken, found me with the knife to my wrist. Two months later, I tried again. At the edge of a cliff, I realized the jagged drop had too many spots to catch my fall. I figured I'd only paralyze myself. I didn't want to explain that in physical therapy.

I stepped into my house, in search of the method. The question hounded me, followed me from room to room. At the kitchen sink, I poured a glass of water and drank the liquid in gulps. Underneath the sink, I eyed my choices. *Liquid-Plumr. Resolve. Tilex.* No, no, that's not it. My prowl for the right means to my end continued. I fingered sharp objects and examined the fine print on medicines new and expired.

Each room presented options, but none felt right. *A fall?* Maybe I could make it look like an accident. Right. Maybe on the first try but not the third.

Unable to end my life, I ran an errand. We needed milk. I drove my car, used my blinker, walked the grocery store aisle, and looked for 2 percent. No one knew; no one asked. *Paper or plastic? Plastic? Would that work? No. Too thin.* I chose paper and pulled out my keys.

On the ride home, I turned off the radio. Focus. One thing at a time. Thoughts strained, as if in need of oxygen. I pulled my car into the garage, discouraged. Then the idea hatched, right as the garage door shut. *Death by carbon monoxide.*

The main garage wouldn't work—too big, too often used. The kids might accidentally interrupt me as they always did when I got on the phone or lifted a fork to my mouth. Death would take less time in the smaller, detached garage. *Relatively painless, no mess, less traumatic for the person who would find me.* This end fit. I felt excited. Done.

The "how" solved, I focused on when, the right moment. Who would find me? Not my kids, no, not my husband, nor my mother. I couldn't let them stumble upon my corpse. This question pursued me like the first.

A door behind me eased open, then shut fast. Margaret's footsteps clicked toward me, heels on tile. Margaret was my helper. Ken hired her months before as our housekeeper, nanny, and mother fill-in for me, the mother impaired.

Yes, she'd be best. No blood relation. In the morning, early, after Ken leaves for work—I can do it then. She smiled at me, her face artfully applied, with every auburn hair magically in place no matter how her head turned. With a tilt of her chin, she asked me if she could do anything to help.

Oh yes, I thought, as I shook my head no.

"Becka, you stand there." Andrew, my seven-year-old son, pointed to the step at the shallow end of the pool. Becka complied, eager for attention from her older brother. Not quite two years apart, these two had reached ages at which they could entertain themselves. They fought but not often. Andrew commanded and Becka followed.

I watched them from the deep end, certain their lives would be better without my presence. Ken surprised us when he came home early from work, no doubt afraid to leave me unsupervised after Margaret clocked out.

He jumped in the water, splattering droplets on the pale sandstone. He swam toward me, underwater, then emerged by my side. We exchanged hellos and a kiss, and he pulled me toward the shallow end, near the kids.

"Make a bridge with your legs, Mommy," Becka commanded. "Let me swim through." I obeyed but felt distant, my isolation magnified at close range. I watched Becka's legs as she kicked beneath me and disappeared.

The conversation stalled. I pulled myself out. Toweling off, I left them without explanation. I needed to see the detached garage, the future place of my permanent disconnection. I planned to kill myself early the next morning after Ken left for work. The kids and my mother would be asleep. Margaret, our housekeeper, would get to work at 8:30 a.m. I wanted to be dead before she arrived.

Death by appointment, the time slot saved.

Our detached garage had become the house closet in those days, piled with stuff I couldn't throw away. We never parked there. At one time, I knew I'd use everything—recycle, reuse, find a purpose. Not that day. I stacked the boxes, arranged the tools, and folded outgrown clothes to make room for my car. The work zoomed by, my actions spurred by conviction I hadn't felt in over a year. When I finished, I brushed myself off and walked back to the pool.

Ken held Becka on his hip while he pitched a Wiffle ball to Andrew in the shallow end. Water baseball. A shot to the hot tub scored an automatic home run. I dove in.

"Where were you?" Ken shouted over his shoulder.

"In the garage." My arms moved in a smooth breaststroke. "Just cleaning up."

"Really?" He smiled. He'd been after me for over a year to straighten that garage. To him, my clean-up seemed a hopeful sign.

After that, I can't recall what happened on my almost-last day on earth. I don't remember my almost-last meal. Astonishing. Though I often forget names, I recollect meals with lustful detail. My mother was visiting. What were my almost-last words to her? What did I say to my children, my husband? Did I make love to my husband?

I don't know.

I was numb, the walking dead, a ghost in a body once vibrant. *Soon, soon, life will be over, soon.* I wanted morning to come fast. No lingering on last meals or last thoughts. I already felt dead. Suffocation began long before the garage door shut.

I poured myself a tumbler of ice water and glanced at the microwave clock. 7:00 a.m. Right on schedule.

My mind felt foggy—like a hangover that never quits. Drugs didn't cause the grogginess; I only used a mild antidepressant. The haze in my brain felt permanent.

I stepped into the main garage, opened the car door, and set my tumbler in the cup holder. My seatbelt fastened, I dug for the keys in my pocket. They jingled. The silver teeth disappeared into the ignition.

My eyes scanned the garage before I turned the key.

Bats and balls littered the corner, and gloves hung on posts for each member of our family of four. Baseball never came easily to me, but my kids caught and threw as if by instinct. They possessed quick reflexes and were calm at the plate. My Rawlings glove dangled from the left peg.

Who will use my glove?

The thought didn't stop me or bring tears to my eyes. Instead, the vision of another reassured me. *I will be replaced. With me gone, my family can heal.*

We stored our sports equipment in the main garage. What a relief. After I was gone, my children wouldn't have to see the spot where I killed myself.

I backed out of the main garage, as I'd done countless times, for carpool, for errands, to volunteer or visit friends. This time, my outing had a final objective. I turned the wheel and pulled into the detached garage. Each panel of the garage door rolled down in my rearview mirror. I let the engine run.

On the dash, the hands of the clock ticked on a face with no numbers.

Will I feel death? Will I just fall asleep? Will I throw up? I imagined the curd-like splatter on the tan upholstery, matted in my straight brown hair. *They won't be able to resell the car.*

The CD flipped to the fourth track.

I put my head on the wheel. *Shouldn't my throat burn? Should the windows be up or down?* They were up. I rolled them down, but it didn't seem to make a difference. I rolled them back up.

"Just be patient," I said. My mother's voice drifted toward me from some far-off place, from a lecture I'd heard throughout adolescence. *Don't always look for immediate gratification.* My own thoughts chimed in, a perfect duet. *Do you think it's going to be easy? What do you expect?*

I want it to stop. I want it over. I'm tired of waiting.

The digital display changed to track eight.

Mom's not warm, but she's not demonic. She's painfully honest. Her bright blue eyes size up the truth quickly, and she delivers her assessment with a sarcastic bite. She's funny, even hysterical, unless the truth has a soft spot. Mom has an Irish wit—fast, lyrical, cutting. I'm often left speechless, admiring the craft of her incision. I often am slow to defend myself verbally, so I write. Hours after the conversation has passed, my comebacks zing. I write these down, in my journal, hoping that next time I can respond in the present tense.

My journal didn't make the trek to the car. No journal. No pen or paper. Typically, I don't sit empty-handed when I have an hour to burn, especially my last one. Usually, at critical junctures I'm scribbling on a page, a stubborn attempt to unwind the knots in my life. Not this time. I didn't have A Reason. There wasn't one reason but a lifetime of reasons. I couldn't fit them in a note.

Track fourteen.

The guitar played, but I felt nothing. Those strums once resonated. Not that morning.

Did I ever feel anything? No. I'm defective. I want life to stop. Why won't life stop? Why won't I stop breathing?

The player was more than halfway through the next CD when I realized the time. I'd been in the garage for over an hour. *Why am I alive?*

Maybe the carbon monoxide isn't getting into the car. I climbed out of the car, engine still engaged, and breathed as deeply as I could. Nothing. I smelled gas, but I felt nothing—no nausea, no head spinning, no fainting with my wrist to my forehead. *What the hell is wrong with me? How long does it take to asphyxiate?*

Margaret's car rolled up outside the garage. Her car door slammed. *How will I explain this?* I heard her heels on the pavement. Her steps faded as she moved away from the garage, toward the house. *Can't she hear the car? Can't she smell something?* Her steps halted. A door opened, shut. She'd entered the house.

I looked at my watch. 8:40. Rage exploded in my chest. *Would you just let me die for Christ's sake?* I kicked a tire. What do you want from me?

I waited. Nothing. No voice from the heavens. No angel of God. No appearance from my dead father. I was alone. The motor droned.

I switched off the engine, rammed the keys into my pocket. Leaving the overhead garage door shut, I opened the side door. The world looked the same. Same concrete, same brick, same unrelenting heat.

"Fuck."

The door slammed behind me as I stepped out into the glaring sun.

2

A Life of Choice

*G*et the door! It's the fish guy," I yell down the stairwell. "I'm on the third floor." I yank on my running tights, grab my shoes, and scramble down the steps of our London row house. That morning in the garage was almost eight years ago. Three months from the London Marathon, I need one long run this week.

"We need some money!" Andrew barks from the ground floor. Dang! I reverse direction, sprint up the stairs. Where the hell did I leave my purse? In the bathroom? I open the door to find Ken at the sink, towel around his waist, shaving.

"Not in here," he shrugs. "Try the kitchen."

Becka's voice floats upward. "Mom, found your wallet. Got twenty pounds. Meet us outside."

I smile. Twelve-year-old Becka handles a twenty-pound note with the confidence of a native. At fourteen, Andrew's mastered the bus system and the multicolored tangle of the Tube. He plays soccer at Regent's Park with his buddies and then heads to Camden Market for Chinese food.

I continue my descent to the ground level. The door hangs open. A blast of cold air reminds me to get my jacket, and I exit. Paul, the fish guy, stands at the back of his truck explaining the options to Andrew and Becka. I move between them, placing a hand on Andrew's shoulder and touching Becka's hair. "What looks good?"

"All of it," Paul says as he sweeps his arm over the fish. "All caught in the last twenty-four hours. Hard to choose."

My stomach growls. Halibut, swordfish, tuna, and salmon all lay on ice, heads off, but cut in massive slabs, which hint at the original size of the fish. I think of the brute strength needed to land all this fish and deliver the catch to my doorstep by 7:30 a.m. My brain fills with options. *Wine sauce, soy, or a lime glaze?*

"Oh, Mom!" Becka points to a thick chunk of whitefish. "Can we get the halibut and make wine sauce with butter and garlic?" She pauses; her tongue grazes her lips. "And mushrooms?"

"Can I eat it raw?" Andrew's discovered sushi and has developed a taste for all things uncooked. Paul's face contorts as he tries to contain his revulsion. I laugh.

"Sure."

"To what?" Becka watches as Paul cuts the slab of halibut into quarter-inch steaks. "Wine sauce or raw?"

"Why not both?" This divide of opinion presents a minor logistical hurdle, one I can hop without effort. "We'll manage."

Our move to London posed daily hurdles, ones that demanded our quick adaptation. At first, the kids railed at every difference. Why is the first floor the "ground floor"? What are trainers? Why are the doorknobs in the center of the door?

Then we encountered the pain of absence. No Diet Dr Pepper. No car, no American football, no cinnamon frosted Pop-Tarts or Andrew's beloved Pepperidge Farm Goldfish.

With absence came that constant, uncomfortable state of new. New school, new friends, new fixtures, new maps in our heads to all the new places. Over time, we all adjusted, me the most willing.

Ken's company needed a London office, so we moved. Some friends thought the move too risky, foolish, an unneeded disruption in our comfortable lives. Switch schools for a year? Live in the drizzle? Leave your friends? Live without a car? We told the kids the news in a restaurant, thinking they wouldn't explode in public. We were wrong.

Becka, normally our calm child, screamed so loud the waiter tried to console her. Her face erupted in waterworks. Andrew reacted with a one-word answer repeated for emphasis, "No. No. No." And then for variety, "No way." The waiter brought our bill early.

We almost didn't move. Gray weather triggered my depression. The thought of the sun setting before 4 p.m. for the month of December frightened me. Reports of cloud-filled skies and fog muffled my enthusiasm. Lack of light combined with two miserable adolescents? No network of friends? Would the suicidal thoughts return?

We decided to take the chance.

I respected my genetic bent for depression but didn't want my identity defined by fear. After radical treatments, psycho-therapy, volumes of writing, and endless discussions about what happened, I knew my tendencies like rote math facts, practiced with flash cards and burned into my brain. The training required a test. If London caused a relapse, I could live through the result. The possibility scared me but didn't lock my feet in the cement of Dallas. Life in a box, afraid of another stint in a psychiatric ward, didn't match my plans.

I left for London with a Seasonal Affective Disorder (SAD) visor and lamp, a full supply of antidepressants, and the name of a psychiatrist in my hip pocket. The visor made me look like a cross between a coal miner with a wayward beacon and an alien tennis player. The box for the SAD hat advertised success with a sunny label but offered no money-back guarantee.

I got on the plane anyway.

The first week, I wondered if I'd made the right choice. Andrew broke down. He missed his friends. He hated his parents for this cultural experience. Becka spent hours and hours on iChat with friends in Dallas. I wondered if she'd ever make a London friend. But within a month, they adjusted.

Andrew starred on the sports teams; Becka spent the night with a new friend. Ken walked more, rode the Tube, and then watched the financial market crash. Although 2008 wasn't Ken's best year, he survived. We learned to trust each other, be tender with each other. Our family grew closer.

We explored new places: Rome, Paris, Amsterdam, Marrakech, Dubai, and Jerusalem. Andrew climbed into a crater from a bomb on the shores of Normandy. Becka climbed Hadrian's Wall and became an expert on ancient flushing toilets.

And me? What did I gain? The best year of my life. I took classes; went to shows, markets, and museums; enjoyed country walks; and went on historical tours. One teacher dubbed me the "culture vulture." With the teacher's insight and the help of *No Fear Shakespeare*, I read the great bard's plays, watched them on the stage, and fell in love with the lyrical sound of his words. I saw Jude Law in *Hamlet* and managed not to drool. With the sound of Big Ben striking, I walked the walk of Mrs. Dalloway. I read Dickens and sat in his seat at the Olde Cheshire Cheese. I took a course in contemporary art and decided I still don't "get" Rothko. Even so, my brain worked and worked well. My year in London ignited my mind; my SAD hat rested on a shelf unused, except on rare occasions. My brain found new light inside my head.

I made friends who changed my life, who helped me believe I could do things I previously thought impossible. I ran a half marathon in Antalya, Turkey, buoyed by the chants of two Turkish runners. At the London Marathon, the crowd cheered my name and toasted me with frothing pints.

On my long training runs, I'd pick out a place I'd never been before, study the map, and then trust my sense of direction. I'd hear languages I couldn't recognize as I traversed parks, ethnic neighborhoods, and the path along the Thames. When I reached my destination, I'd catch the Tube back home to St. John's Wood. Later in the day, the kids walked home from school, the Abbey Road crossing part of their daily routine. I'd ask them what happened during their days, and they'd tell me "nothing."

"Nothing? Really?"

"Really, nothing."

Some things don't change, even with a change in continents. Becka and I made dinner—always fish on Wednesday, fresh off the back of Paul's truck.

If I had taken my life, none of this would've happened. Even without a George-Bailey-It's-a-Wonderful-Life visit from an angel, I can imagine the lives of my husband, children, family, and friends if my life had ended on that hot summer day.

Instead, I chose to live.

Sometimes that's all life needs to unfold its abundance—a choice, a decision, or a movement into the unknown. My first step was shaky. I couldn't see eight years into the future. I didn't believe I'd get better, but I took the first step anyway. I got lucky. My deathtrap brain failed to truncate my existence. I stepped through the door. Life unfolded. The next step led to an adventure an ocean away, far from the coffin of my own garage.

Paul hands Becka the halibut, sliced and wrapped in white paper. We scramble back into the house, Andrew first, pushed by Becka, followed by me. I shut the door on the cold, damp air and walk into the well-lit kitchen. I put the fish in the refrigerator and glance at the vegetables, making a mental list of the items we need for the evening's meal.

Ken strolls down the stairs. "What did you buy? Something good?"

"Fresh halibut." Mushrooms, white wine, garlic, and butter—I imagine the ingredients in a sauce my senses can't resist. I close the door, turn toward Ken, and plant a morning kiss on his lips.

"What's the occasion? All this over fresh fish?"

I nod. I grab my pen and write down the shopping list. "I can already taste the butter."

3

Trust in a Different Map

You need to consider ECT." Dr. Galen uncrossed his long legs and glanced at Ken.

Ken breathed out while Artie, my psychologist, breathed in. My stint in the garage bought me an emergency visit with my psychiatrist, who managed my medications; my psychologist, with whom I did talk therapy; and my husband, who was at his wit's end.

After I marched out of the garage on that hot August morning, I stepped into my house, baffled that ninety minutes hadn't done the trick. Why didn't my suicide attempt work? A house builder friend claims the vaulted roof above the garage ceiling saved my life. The architecture provided ventilation that kept the carbon monoxide from building up. I told Margaret about the attempt immediately. I'm not sure why. After a scramble of phone calls—Margaret to Ken, Ken to Artie, Artie to Dr. Galen, Dr. Galen to Ken—I found myself in Dr. Galen's office with my trio of caretakers. They surrounded me, leaning forward in their seats. I was the patient, often discussed in third person, the "she" who attempted, who appeared resistant to medication, whose thoughts of suicide transformed into action. The she who needed ECT.

Dr. Galen looked like a praying mantis, limbs too long for his body, and his tiny head perched with a sensitive twist. A tall man, a physical force but gentle. Kind, someone to be trusted. His oversized, out-of-date glasses magnified his eyes. This man wanted to help me. I knew that, despite the terror inspired by a three-letter abbreviation.

ECT.

Dr. Galen explained electroconvulsive therapy. The information shot straight to my stomach, twisting like an undigested cut of beef. Visions of *One Flew Over the Cuckoo's Nest* and Jack Nicholson danced in my head. Nicholson writhed, a rag stuffed in his mouth; he shook uncontrollably. The image had stayed with me for more than twenty years. In the movie, the doctor flipped the switch and lost his humanity in the strength of his fingertips. Now I had to trust my doctor, whose fingers would release that same burst of electricity throughout my brain.

Mind control, thought control; ECT tapped my dread of a *Brave New World*. I'd seen one woman's reaction to ECT in my last overnight stay in the Zale Lipshy hospital psychiatric ward, five months prior, right after my first suicide attempt. The woman, Gladys, paced in group therapy. Her red hair stood in tufts. "I've got no reason to be here," she said, "no reason to be depressed." She couldn't remember her doctor's name five seconds after we told her. I feared I'd be like her—unable to control myself, completely dependent on the judgment of others.

Ken cleared his throat. The sound startled me, brought me back to my circle of caretakers who waited for my decision.

I looked down, felt their eyes on the top of my head. "I need to think."

On the ride home, Ken wanted my answer. I looked out the window.

"Well?" Ken turned toward me, eyes off the road. Early in our marriage, I'd slam the imaginary brake through the floor when Ken drove too fast. After eleven years, I'd learned to steady my foot.

"The road—"

"What?"

"Can you keep your eyes—"

"Jesus! You're trying to kill yourself but worry about my driving? Do you see anything wrong with this?"

"The kids need you."

He softened, stared ahead. "They need both of us. I need you. I can't do this alone."

How could he think he needed me? For nine months, negative thoughts had consumed my brain. We tried therapy and drugs. He sent me away for a month to anti-depression camp. He hired people to help and enlisted the help of friends. None of his arsenal worked.

"You think I'll get better." I glanced at Ken, then stared out the windshield. "But this is who I am. This is who I've always been."

Ken drove with one hand on the wheel, green eyes fixed on white lines as they flashed past.

"Julie, this isn't you. It's your depression talking."

I hated that expression. It sounded like some pop-psych sound bite. Almost as bad as "suicide is a permanent solution to a temporary problem."

Ken worked through his points methodically. "You love life more than anyone I know."

Did I? Life didn't feel so lovable. Depression didn't feel like something but rather the absence of any feeling. Flat. Disconnected.

"I can't keep faking," I mumbled. We spent so much time and money on my elusive recovery. "There's someone else for you . . ." The person they wanted was an act I couldn't sustain. "You're young . . . rich . . . plenty of women will want to marry you."

Ken pounded the steering wheel and swerved. The man in the battered white Chevy Impala next to us snarled and flipped me off. I pretended he didn't exist.

"How can I make you see?" The veins stood out on Ken's neck.

"I see myself . . . for the first time in my life."

Ken rolled his eyes. "And the kids? Are *they* better off without you?"

I thought about this for a second. "Yes."

Ken breathed in, out. In. Out. As if he were trying to pace himself. Ken didn't explode when he got angry, at least not with me. He got silent. He leaned back in his seat and straightened his shoulders.

"You have two choices. Do ECT, or I go. I can't take it anymore."

I hated him for this. Backed into a corner, I had to say yes. My depression-controlled brain reasoned my children could weather my suicide but not a divorce.

"Okay. I'll do ECT."

Ken nodded. He knew not to talk past the sale.

When we got home, Andrew and Becka ran toward Ken. He swung one, then the other high into the air. My children peered at me like an unwanted relative who entered their house. I'm sure they were confused—I had the same body as the mom who took them to the zoo, played baseball, and rolled out yard-long sheets of butcher paper for a spontaneous mural, but now I was different. Breakable.

"Hi, Mommy." Becka took my hand. "Want to play Clue Jr.?"

"Okay." I squeezed her hand. She let go and bounded up the stairs.

My footsteps sounded heavy on the stairs, thuds on carpet, steps absent springs. At the top of the stairs, I turned into the playroom. They'd set the board in the center of a table, the pieces at the starting point.

"This game is for babies," Andrew spat.

"You said . . . ," Becka fired back.

"Did not. Dad made me play. Mom doesn't want to play either."

They didn't seem to notice me. "I'll play, Becka."

Their heads turned in my direction, perplexed. They hadn't noticed my presence. That happened often.

"Okay, Mommy, let's play." Becka handed me a card and a pencil.

She rolled the die, and the game began. I made every possible mistake. The die flew off the table. I moved the piece in the wrong direction, miscounted the spaces on the board. Becka corrected me first with patience, then with a glare—a spotlight on my stupidity. The game went on and on. For some reason, the location eluded us. Becka, a champion at this game, couldn't understand our inability to solve the puzzle.

"Lay down your cards," she said. "Maybe we forgot something."

I obeyed, spreading my cards on the table.

"Mommy! Right there—you cheated!" She pointed to the tree house card in my hand.

I picked up the evidence of my incompetence. *How did I miss that?*

"I asked you! My first question—you cheat!"

My thoughts churned through the questions of the game. I heard our voices, back and forth. The scratches on my detective sheet, haphazard, gave me no clue as to places I'd eliminated. When I glanced up, Becka was gone.

I picked up the box. Appropriate for ages four to six. *How can I raise kids when I can't play Clue Jr.?*

When I looked up again, Andrew stood in the doorway.

"What's wrong with you?" he asked. My mouth moved but nothing came out. He shook his head and turned away.

The next few weeks were painful. Airplanes crashed into the Twin Towers, the Pentagon, and a field in western Pennsylvania a few days before I entered the locked psychiatric ward. While the rest of the world gaped in horror, I nodded. The inside of my head kept playing on television screens over and over again. Crash, burn, collapse. Crash. Burn. Collapse. As others mourned the deaths, I wished I were one of the victims.

Let me trade places.

Did God bargain with suicidal women? The victims' families needed them. *I'm damaging mine.* I watched the black specks leap from buildings. *Save them, not me.*

At Zale Lipshy, my initial ECT treatments were scheduled as inpatient, to be administered on Monday, Wednesday, and Friday. If I dramatically improved, they would consider doing the next three sessions outpatient. After that, the treatments would be spread out— two a week, then once a week, until we'd completed eight to twelve sessions.

Ken went with me to check in Sunday night. When we reached Zale Lipshy, we took the elevator up to the fourth floor, to the locked door of the psychiatric ward. We rang the buzzer.

The door unnerved me; it stood as a boundary, separating the sane· from the insane, distinguishing reality from the altered state my mind had invented. A stay in a locked ward proved that I was out of control and out of my mind; and I had to trust that someone else could care for me better than I could care for myself.

A doctor opened the door, met us in the hall, and explained the process for checking into the psycho hotel. Texas state law required a patient to sign a consent document before entering a psychiatric ward. The document ensured the patient wasn't forced to enter and allowed the facility to hold the patient until danger passed. The doctor gave me a moment to read the form and then handed me a pen.

"I can't do this." I pushed the paper away. *What if Ken decides to put me away for good?*

Or worse, I feared I'd spend the rest of my life vacant, like Gladys from group therapy, after her session of ECT. Unable to think or make decisions, dependent on others—this wasn't a life I wanted. *I'd rather be dead.*

I handed the form back to the doctor, walked toward the elevator. I pressed the down button, Ken on my heels. When the elevator opened, he pulled at my arm, but I unhooked myself and stepped inside. Ken followed. The doors shut.

"You have to do this." Ken talked while the floors ticked down, listing the reasons for ECT. "You promised."

I counted the seconds until the doors opened. "I need some air." Down the hall, I pushed the glass door open into the parking lot. Heat rose from the asphalt. Cars raced past on the expressway.

"Do we need provisions?" Ken liked a Diet Dr Pepper and something loaded with sugar for his walks with me. He never knew when a walk would turn into a longer excursion.

I shook my head no.

"Fine. I'm going to run inside and get something." He turned toward the building.

My throat tightened. "No, don't leave me." I did this often—push away and pull back. Ken's presence irritated me, but his absence terrified me.

Ken breathed out. "Well, I'm thirsty. I'm going in."

"Wait. Okay, I'll sign." I realized I wouldn't escape ECT. I had to trust Dr. Galen. I had to trust Ken. I had to trust that I was the person everyone told me I was. I had to trust the outside world more than my own brain.

"Let's go." I took Ken's hand, ready to lie to ease his conscience. "I feel better."

That's how I remember the day—one trip down, two trips up, the second time with provisions. Ken says that we made that trip up and down the elevator several times. I didn't want to sign those papers or to walk through that door. I signed anyway and entered the locked ward.

The psychiatric ward wasn't nearly as frightening on the other side of the locked door. The nurse checked me into the ward. I had met LaTisha during my first visit to the psychiatric ward, five months earlier, after my first suicide attempt.

LaTisha wasn't much taller than me but probably outweighed me by forty pounds. She wasn't fat; I was pencil thin. I didn't eat when I was depressed, an instant weight-loss program with shocking results. I didn't consciously deprive myself of food. I just had no appetite. During a physical a few months before, my doctor accused me of being anorexic. She informed me that only gymnasts have less than 11 percent body fat.

LaTisha swallowed me with her hug, her cornrows swinging as she moved. "Back so soon? That's okay, girl, we're gonna fix you up good this time."

Her words comforted me, made me relax, perhaps because she seemed to be the only one who believed I'd recover. Ken, Dr. Galen, and Artie suggested a route of best probability, but the risk and their fear showed. LaTisha knew as though she had already seen me well, a whole person.

LaTisha showed me to my room, with Ken following. He wrapped his arms around me. "I love you. Thank you for being so brave."

Brave? I didn't feel brave. Trapped, yes. Terrified, yes, but not brave.

"Are you going to be okay?"

I nodded. I looked at the ceiling. I summoned a prayer from my childhood. *Hail Mary, full of grace, the Lord is with thee . . . what came next?* I counted the ceiling tiles. *I can still count, right? One, two . . .*

Blessed are women? Blessed art thou? Ken couldn't help me now. I pushed him away, told him to take care of the kids. He squeezed my hand and walked down the hall. The exit door opened, and he stepped through. The door shut. The lock clicked.

I headed toward the social room for the ward, a spacious area with floor-to-ceiling windows and a grand piano in the corner. On the opposite end of the room, a wall of windows lined the command center, buzzing with nurses, doctors, and techs, as well as whiteboards with schedules, medication, and a bank of cell phones, all charging, their cords under strict supervision. A cell phone cord became a noose in the wrong hands.

I wandered toward some chairs near the piano. I sat next to an attractive blonde, makeup applied, probably in her thirties. She cut off her conversation to the woman next to her as soon as I sat down.

"You look normal," she said. "Are you a patient or staff?"

"Patient."

"You're sure?"

"Yes, I'm sure."

"Good. You're not a spy." She turned and finished her conversation with the woman next to her. "We're making friggin' trivets. Who the hell needs a trivet?" She leaned toward me.

"Cathy." She extended her hand. Cathy tossed her long hair over her shoulder and took a sip of her Diet Coke.

"Julie. You look normal too."

She laughed, and I smiled back.

"What's your problem?" I looked for scars, clues.

"Manic . . . manic-depressive. Oh, wait, the last place I went they didn't call it that. Bipolar. Sounds much better." The words came out like machine-gun fire.

"Last place?"

"Menningers, Sierra Tucson, I'm a true wacko professional. Just keep screwing up. Wrecked my car this time. Drunk. My two kids in the back."

"I tried to kill myself." My words came out calmly, easily, as if I were telling her my address.

"No shit?" Cathy paused, took another gulp.

I nodded.

"That's bad. You got kids?"

"Two. A boy and a girl. Seven and five."

"So what will you try? Lithium? That works for me sometimes."

"No. ECT." I looked down at the silver legs of the chair. "But I might not do it." Ken had walked out that door. It was my life now. I still wasn't sure.

"Why not?"

"I saw this woman once, Gladys, last time I was here. She looked so fried—"

"But not dead," Cathy added.

"No, not dead, but she didn't even know her name. I don't want to live like that."

Cathy interrogated me about every drug and therapy I'd tried. For someone who talked so fast, she listened better than I anticipated. When I finished, she told me about Gerald, another patient on the floor who had ECT fourteen years earlier and was back after a depression relapse.

"ECT worked for him," she said. "Check it out."

"Worked? He's back in the loony bin."

"He got fourteen years more of life, and he made it back here."

I grunted, "Great life, in and out of the nuthouse."

"It's a tune-up!" Cathy's voice boomed. "He could go another fourteen without trouble." She folded her arms across her chest. "Hell, would you rather be dead or give your children a mother?"

I wasn't sure.

"Isn't it better for them if you live?"

"I don't know . . . ," I exhaled. "What if I'm screwing them up? I might be harming them. Not feeding them right, stunting their growth—"

"Jesus, you are crazy. You're not beating them, right?"

"No!"

"Then how could you believe they would be better off?" Cathy presented the perfect argument. She crunched the Diet Coke can, wobbled it back and forth. A few drops fell on her jeans. "Would you rather be short or think your mother loved you so little that she killed herself?" She wiped the drops away.

"But they're better off with me gone."

Cathy grabbed me by the arms and gave me a little shake to make me look her in the face. "They'll never believe that, even if it's true."

I looked away from her. I knew she was right, but I didn't want to hear her. I was so tired.

"What if ECT screws me up? What if I can't remember?"

"You got two babies at home," she said. "I'll help you when you come out. I'll tell you who you are. But you gotta do it, girl."

"Okay, okay." I brushed her away. "I'll talk to Gerald."

Gerald owned a plumbing business and his company serviced over fifty apartment complexes. Gerald appeared to be in his mid-sixties. His wife died. A year later he almost lost his business. He didn't care if all the toilets in the Terrace Apartments overflowed on the same day. He'd crawl in the back room behind his office where he kept a cot, pull the blanket over his head, and go to sleep. When his psychiatrist suggested ECT, he thought the doctor was crazy. Even so, he relented and did eight sessions of ECT. "I was enthusiastic about life again. I wanted to do things, to try new ideas. My smile lit up like a light bulb."

While Gerald didn't look like a poster boy for health, he believed in ECT. I returned to my room frightened but hopeful. I lay on the bed and closed my eyes. What a concept—enthusiastic about life.

Unable to rest, I picked up my journal. I wrote about Gerald. I believed ECT worked for him—but for me? Doubt hit the page. What if I got worse?

I'd seen the statistics. ECT had a better and faster success rate than any antidepressant. I'd read Martha Manning's *Undercurrents*. Manning did ECT and recovered. She seemed like me—same religious origin, a mother, and busy. Cratered by depression but then cured. Could I be like her? ECT felt so random, the success inexplicable, the process so barbaric.

I had to turn my brain off. Dr. Galen, my family, and some of my friends pointed to ECT, a path they believed led to my health. Could I trust their map? No one guaranteed recovery. I wanted a fail-proof method but only got a procedure that might work. I had to trust. I shut my journal, set down my pen.

4

ECT

*F*our empty, portable hospital beds lined the wall the next morning. Three of us stood against the opposite wall, afraid our hospital gowns might gap in the back, revealing old boxers or worn lingerie.

Gerald strolled up to me and touched my shoulder. Our last names and first initials showed in green lettering on the whiteboard near the room where they administered the shocks. Gerald smiled. "Looks like I'm numero uno."

He hopped on the first bed, stretched out, put his hands behind his head. "It'll be okay. By lunch you'll be chomping on fried chicken wondering what you were afraid of." Gerald shimmied in the bed for a better fit. "What'd you pick?"

The three of us stood against the wall, lost in our own thoughts.

"Julie. For lunch? What'd ya pick for lunch?"

I blinked my eyes. The attendant handed me a menu the night before, but my choice eluded me. *If my memory is this bad before ECT, what will happen afterward?*

"Hey kid, it's only lunch, not life and death." Gerald grinned. For a depressed guy, he seemed pretty damn happy.

"Life and death?" LaTisha appeared from around the corner. "Gerald, what are you trying to do to this girl?" LaTisha guided me to the second bed. "Can't you see she's scared out of her mind?"

"Looks like she's in the right place." Gerald chuckled. "She's gonna be okay, you know that."

"I do, but she don't." LaTisha pulled a blanket from underneath the bed. "Have a little mercy." She pulled the blanket up to my neck. She turned to the other two patients.

"Come on, you two. Miss Judith, you're three." LaTisha led the thin, frail woman to the third bed and helped her get settled. "Carson, you're four," LaTisha called over her shoulder. "Get yourself up there."

Carson snorted. "Can't I get a smoke first?"

LaTisha glared at him. "What'd you think?"

Carson said something under his breath. The stench of the last smoke break followed him. When he hopped on the bed, the metal frame banged against the wall.

"Watch it, will you?" LaTisha scowled. "Some folks are still sleeping."

Another attendant appeared. He'd taken my vitals the day before. "Hey, Tisha, we're behind. We gotta get these beds rolling."

"We're ready, we're ready." LaTisha positioned Judith's blanket. "Take Gerald, he's good to go."

"Let's move," Gerald said. "I'm ready for a quick sleep."

"Okay, man, let's roll." The attendant pushed the bed out into the hallway.

"What're ya having for lunch? What'd ya think—" Gerald's voice disappeared through the swinging double doors.

Will this make me better? I thought of Manning's book. She was a good Catholic girl. She counted her rosary beads and said a Hail Mary to block her suicidal thoughts. *Will I be like her?*

I couldn't call myself a Catholic anymore; I was a FARC at best— Fallen Away Roman Catholic. Disgusted with the Catholic Church, I'd stopped going about twenty years ago. But some things stick. The words came back easily, as if I'd said them every day of my life.

Our Father, who art in heaven.

LaTisha appeared at my side. "Okay, Miss Julie, it's your turn."

I nodded. *Hallowed be thy name.*

The doctors filed into the room. The anesthesiologist chatted with me, told me not to be afraid as the nurse placed the electrodes on my chest.

"We do this to monitor heart rate, to make sure you're steady through the procedure."

Thy kingdom come. Thy will be done.

Dr. Galen appeared. The nurse spread a gel on each electrode, a quarter-sized silver disk, and placed one on each temple. The anesthesiologist joked, checked the syringes with the various medications. I lay back on the table, and the nurse strapped my arms and legs in place in case the muscle relaxant failed to stop the spasms. Dr. Galen put his hand on my right arm.

"Are you ready for this?"

I shook my head no, then yes. *On earth as it is in heaven.*

"Julie, you'll live, I promise."

But what kind of life? Who will I be after the lightning storm? I had to trust him, but I can't remember another moment in my life when I felt so afraid, so alone. My lips moved without sound as anesthetic surged into my veins. *Lead us not into temptation, but deliver us from evil.*

I blinked. Light assaulted my eyes. *Where was I? Who was I?*

A woman helped me off the bed and held my arm as I walked to the door. Her nametag formed a connection for my brain. *LaTisha.* Nurse. Gold tooth. Sharps.

Another woman met us as we walked into the social room—thick blonde hair, makeup expertly applied. She grabbed my face in her two hands.

"You're Julie Hersh, you have two kids, Andrew seven, Becka five."

"What the hell are you doing!" LaTisha pushed the woman aside.

I held up my hand. "It's okay, okay." The two of them looked at me, surprised. They probably didn't think I could say anything so quickly, less than an hour after the procedure. "I told her to tell me who I am."

LaTisha shook her head and sat me down in the chair. "Whatever. Just don't fall over."

The woman claimed the seat next to me and continued to fill me in. "You're married to Ken, you live in Dallas—"

"Texas?"

"Yes, Texas!" She clapped her hands.

"Who are you again?" I knew I should know her, but I couldn't remember her name.

"Cathy, remember? We met yesterday."

I did. I remembered.

Cathy held my hand for the next hour. She reminded me that Gerald encouraged me the day before, about how scared I was. Hopeless. Illogical.

"You weren't making any sense at all." She spoke as though my problems were past. I felt calm. Not fearless, not confused, just calm.

Finally I went back to my room, picked up my journal, and read the last entry.

The words confirmed what I knew—even after just one treatment, I was better. I'd finally surfaced on the other side of a wave that had swallowed me for nine months. My depression had trapped me in a watery cage for so long I no longer knew where or how to find air. Psychological vertigo. Death had been certain, inevitable, and imminent. Finally, I burst through the water, salt on my lips, salt of tears I'd been unable to cry. In an instant, I could breathe again.

Most people don't have this level of response with one ECT treatment. Typically, patients require six to ten sessions for a sustained lift of depression. A few people, like me, feel instantly better. Often, family and staff notice a positive change before the depressed person can feel the change herself. For me, one treatment completely changed my perspective.

I made phone calls I don't remember, one of the costs of running electricity through a stubborn brain. Ken told me I called him on the golf course, the spark in my voice noticeable for the first time in nine months.

My mother said she talked to me and cried afterward, relieved her child had returned. I'm sure I spoke with my children, but they were too young to remember, unaware of how different their lives might've been if this option, along with the others, had failed. My life didn't magically realign, but I no longer felt I deserved a death sentence.

The next morning I woke up sore—my neck, shoulders, jaws, and legs all ached. LaTisha assured me that the pain was normal and would subside and that I'd probably have a headache. I did.

I felt tired but optimistic, positive enough to notice the clear blue skies and view of downtown Dallas from my window. My journal shows I could finally feel again, noticing others, empathizing with their pain. The cage that had enclosed me, allowing me to see the world but not touch or feel, was gone.

My closing words of that day's journal entry summed up my life in that moment: Now I can rest.

With the help of Cathy, Gerald, the staff, and doctors, I began to piece together my identity. The memories weren't lost, just the connections to the memories. My memories floated like islands in my head. The ECT shook the bridges to those islands like an earthquake. Some bridges crashed and required new building. Some bridges just needed reinforcement. Some events, in the weeks immediately before and after ECT, were gone forever. Most of the moments immediately before ECT I'd like to forget anyway. The moments lost after, I consider a small surcharge. ECT, primitive as it seems, saved my life.

Ken brought me lunch that afternoon and visited the next morning, but I have no recollection of his visit. My running partner Kate came by two days later. Kate, dressed in her pressed khaki shorts and white cotton golf shirt and sporting a tan, appeared out of place on the locked ward. Her eyes wandered to all the strange sights to which I'd become accustomed.

A large muscular man across the room erupted every twenty minutes or so about his dick or her cunt. Another patient, a woman, slammed him back in his place with one comment: "John, don't be such a prick." John withered.

My friend Kate ate her salad, eyes fixed on her plate. She looked up with brows raised high. "It's okay," I mouthed.

Verbal eruptions were commonplace in the psychiatric ward, as people addressed each other without the boundaries of appropriate conversation. I looked from John the prick, to the woman, to my friend Kate. When Kate averted her eyes, I understood how she felt. But for me, the ward felt comfortable, a place where I fit.

People talked about suicide, incest, death, drugs, and alcoholism in the locked ward the way buddies chat about their golf games in the bar after a round. I guess that's why the ward's locked and they check for sharps at the door.

Still, I felt at home there. Once I talked with the people on the ward, their actions made more sense. The difference between them and me was a difference of degree. Maybe I got help sooner, maybe I had help from friends and family, or maybe I possessed the income for better treatment.

The mind is a fragile thing, so unpredictable. What is crazy? Why do people go crazy? I can't answer that question. I only know that when a brain is compromised, with the right set of circumstances, anyone is vulnerable.

Kate feared the inside of the ward. I feared the world outside. *What would happen when I exited?* The ward was a cocoon, a place where whatever I said would be tolerated and where someone else controlled my schedule. On Wednesday, Kate asked if I counted the days until Friday, the day of my final release.

I did. But for different reasons than she thought.

I felt safe behind that locked door.

Ken took me home on Friday. No journal entry for that day, most of the day's memories lost. I do remember returning to my bedroom at home, the afternoon sun pouring through the cream sheers. The same scene looked different a week earlier, artificial, uncomfortable, and pretentious. Post-ECT, I marveled at the light.

I sat on the cushy chair, ran my hand across the fabric, and put my feet on the ottoman. Andrew's steps pattered on the wooden hallway outside my door. He laughed. I hugged him tightly when he entered the room.

"Want to go swimming?" he asked.

"Of course."

How could life feel so different? But it did. Life felt very different.

I continued outpatient treatment on Monday and Wednesday of the following week and felt increasingly better. I took Becka to the State Fair of Texas that week and navigated the crowds and food lines, something I would've been terrified to do two weeks before. My world was different. I saw the same world but with new eyes.

ECT helped my mood, no question, but I became confused and forgetful after every treatment. Once, I drove to the end of the street headed to the YMCA. I'd coached at the YMCA, been to hundreds of soccer games and practices. When I reached the stop sign, my mind went blank. I willed myself to recall the directions. Finally, five minutes later, the next step emerged. *Turn left.* Once I remembered that step, the rest of the directions flowed. The bridge connected to the island in my head. I knew the way.

This doesn't seem so bad, except as a mother of two small children, there were lots of islands for the small things—the way to the grocery store, where to look for lost toys, the route to friends' houses. The minutes in limbo, when I waited for the bridges to be reconstructed, added up.

I'd begin to have some clarity and then go in for another ECT treatment. The bridges would crash, and I'd lose the map to those islands in my head. I remained calm, but reconstruction was frustrating.

Ken encouraged me, but I felt like an idiot. My children probably didn't understand how Mommy could get so mixed up. Other mommies didn't sit so long at stop signs, always talking to themselves—"Okay, think. Come on. You can do it."

After the first five treatments, I wanted to stop. I felt I'd derived the benefits from the procedure, and I no longer wanted to deal with the disorientation after each treatment. ECT hobbled me in daily life.

Dr. Galen was on vacation, so I called the acting psychiatrist to drop the next treatment. The psychiatrist assured me that with the treatments spread further apart, my memory problems would dramatically decrease. I didn't buy it. I told the doctor I felt much better and would continue taking my antidepressant but needed to stop ECT treatments.

"No, you can't possibly do that." The cadence and volume of the doctor's voice increased. "Percentages show that almost everyone falls back into depression if they don't perform the normally scheduled treatments." His voice held panic—interesting to hear in someone's voice besides my own.

"I understand the downside, but can you show me a study that defines the percentages?" My voice stayed even.

"What?" Obviously this doctor wasn't accustomed to his depressed patients demanding statistics.

"What are my risks? Do I have an 80 percent chance of recurrence?"

"Well—"

"Sixty? Twenty? I just to need to know." Driving the wrong way down a one-way street while rebuilding my mental bridges might be dangerous too.

"I'm sure those numbers are somewhere." He paused. "Look, you have to listen to me. You can't just stop. I can't be responsible for what might happen."

"I'm not asking you to be responsible." For the first time in a long time, I liked the sound of my voice. "I just want the facts." I sounded like the old me and a new me at the same time.

I refused further ECT treatments.

When Dr. Galen got back a week later, we talked over my options. He told me no study definitively linked a more frequent recurrence of depression if the patient did at least six ECT treatments and continued other forms of therapy. If the patient dropped everything—ECT, psychotherapy, and medication—the chance of relapse was high. "As high as 80 percent in six months."

Dr. Galen felt that even with only five treatments, as long as I took medication and continued psychotherapy and we both monitored my behavior carefully, my chances were as good as continuing with more ECT. The choice was up to me. I was back in charge.

Back in charge. I liked the sound of that.

5

Back in Charge

*T*he numbers glowed past Ken's rumpled pillow. 3:30. I turned on my side, counted the hours of sleep in my head. Four. Five the night before, three and a half the night before that. *I've got to sleep.* I closed my eyes, waited, and then looked at the clock again. 3:35.

I edged out of the covers and traversed the dark hallways of my house like a thief. My brain, already in a sprint, calculated all the things I could do in the four hours before carpool—plan menus for the week, check e-mails, get back to a friend about the spiritual rift between my Christian roots and Judaism, outline my book for Rashmi, organize photographs, and make a grocery list.

I flicked on my computer with the certainty of an illusionist ready to pull off a well-practiced trick. My fingers hit the keyboard, paragraphs spilling out.

"What the hell are you doing?" Ken's voice jolted me midsentence.

"Just a little work. Did I wake you? I'm sorry."

Ken rubbed his forehead. "It's 5:30. How long have you been up?"

"Oh, I don't know." I glanced at my computer. When did I send the messages? Would he see the time stamp? "A half-hour?"

Ken grunted, shook his head. "You're lying—you were long gone by five. Your side of the bed was cold."

I got out of my chair and brushed past him. "Who are you? The police?" I exited my office. "I'm finally better, and you're all over me."

He strode after me, grabbed my wrist. "Slow down."

I turned, shoved away his hand. "I'm not like you. I don't have an assistant—this is the only time of day I can work."

"Do you want to end up back there? I can't take another breakdown. You're gonna burn yourself out—"

"I'm not sick anymore! Do you hear me—when are you going to trust me?"

Ken stepped forward. I could feel his breath. "When you stop lying."

I returned his glare, then sputtered, "I have to get dressed."

"It's five-fucking-thirty!"

I turned away from him and walked down the hall to our room. "I'm going for a run."

"Fine," he called after me, "run away."

After ECT, I raced back into life, zero to sixty, within days. Dr. Galen sent me home, prescribing an antidepressant and a weekly checkup with him, as well as a weekly counseling session with my psychologist, Artie. I kept the appointments and took the medicine. I didn't like it. My psychological maintenance felt like a choke collar, tightening around my throat each time I sprang forward.

I spent a full year under strict supervision of doctors, family, and friends. I wanted my life back. I took the steering wheel and slammed down the accelerator. My velocity of recovery made everyone nervous. Their caution seemed skittish from my perspective, a vote of no confidence in my obvious recovery. In Ken's eyes, I saw my reflection as the mentally altered, the one lacking in judgment. I resented that role. Our relationship felt uncomfortable, a straitjacket imposed by a patronizing spouse.

Even as I sparred with Ken about the validity of the new me, I had my own doubts. With ECT, I felt better almost instantly. Why? How could I want to kill myself one day, not as a passing thought but as an obsession, and the next day understand the futility of suicide? I had the same life, the same body, even the same mind. What caused my depression? Hormones? Some brain chemical malfunction? Genetic disposition? I couldn't ask these questions and not face the hardest one.

Will it happen again?

Although the questions were daunting, I was determined to guard my life against recurrence. I had the energy to lead the attack. One of the side effects of ECT, at least in my case, was a six-week period of "hypomania." I didn't like Dr. Galen's term, preferring instead to think of the change as happy Julie versus depressed Julie.

I was tireless, up at 3:30 a.m. and charged until midnight; I wrote missive e-mails, transported children, bought golf clubs, found Halloween decorations, had lunch with my husband, coached soccer, took photos, gave edicts, created a life plan with bullet points, talked, read, cheered at soccer games, attended school functions, prepared meals, maintained a house, set up a new allowance structure for the kids, and crashed after a seventeen-hour day, then woke up at 3:30 a.m. for a repeat performance the following day. Life lived as one long run-on sentence. I thought I was amazing. Ken described me as a rat on crack.

I have days jammed with action now, as mentally stable people do, but they exhaust me. Many of us are propelled by caffeine and an overbooked schedule. The difference rests in a natural flow of energy. When I was manic, the relationship between energy and activity became skewed. The more I did, the more wired I became. There was no rest, no downtime. The more I did, the more convinced I became of my invincibility, my infallibility, and my own magical power.

I jumped into dozens of activities at once, with the enthusiasm of a lifelong passion but the focus of a gnat. I wrote. My pen attacked pages with zeal. I prayed and joined an Episcopal church. To stimulate my hidden talents, I took an art class and practiced piano with Becka. I played golf and ran at least four miles most days. Motherhood remained critical. I initiated new rules for my children: less TV, more reading, soccer skills training, a chores list. Everything collided at the top of my list, a number one priority.

I threw parties and had a knack for initiating profound discussions with near strangers who I treated as intimate friends. In my spare time, usually between the hours of 4 a.m. and 6 a.m., I wrote a detailed outline for a case study about depression recovery. I wrote deep, long e-mails, self-absorbed, navel-gazing stuff that would never survive an editor's cut. I did all these things in about six weeks.

I've maintained some of these activities and a few of these friendships, but despite my sincere intentions, most of these ideas remained ideas. At best, they were seeds spread with frantic desire, without sunlight or sufficient water to take root. The chores checklist, incomplete and unchecked, hung on Andrew's bulletin board for years.

During my frenetic period, I met weekly with Artie, my psychologist. Intellectually, I accepted the need for psychotherapy. Today, the only measure of progress in mental illness is the patient's behavior and attitude, which is often difficult to gauge. Dr. Galen couldn't scan my brain and point out areas that had recovered or still needed healing. He studied me in a psychiatric ward and observed changes, but reintegration into my world was completely different. Psychotherapy provided a benchmark to determine if my mental health slipped or remained on track.

One side of my brain accepted psychotherapy. The other side tallied all the hours consumed by therapy when I already felt better. Emotionally, psychotherapy felt like weights on my sprinter's build. I had no desire to have someone else peruse my life and pick out all the bad parts.

Artie weathered the worst of my depression with me. He lasted through my first suicide venture, my first stay at Zale Lipshy, and my attempt in the garage. He endured ECT by my side. Artie was always there, unfailingly. I could call him anytime of the day and expect immediate response, even a drive-by emergency visit if necessary. Post-ECT, Artie provided something that was critical to my recovery: another set of eyes to monitor my progress.

Artie had a kind heart. He held his sessions in his home, a dimly lit place with a Zen-like quality. A cold Fresca always awaited me, as well as a thickly padded chair. About twenty years my senior, Artie had far more life experience. A few months after ECT, however, our meetings forged more consternation than consolation. The man seemed inordinately focused on my relationship with my mother.

As I thought about the future, I wondered if Artie would be the right person to guide me. Being forty-one and married, I saw big emotional challenges: balancing my desires with my relationships and looming menopause. Artie had no children, had been divorced more than once, and was male. Artie gained his wisdom vicariously, through past clients and books. I wanted someone who had lived the life I wanted. Artie helped me through the roughest part of my depression, his accessibility and support saving me on several occasions. For that, I was grateful. With his help, I stood at a new phase of recovery, one that required me to leave him behind.

The job description for the perfect counselor formed in my head like a help wanted ad: "Experienced psychologist needed. Must speak and understand women's needs. Proven long-term marriage, menopause survivor. References from children and husband must be available on request. Cash incentive for outstanding work and early client self-awareness."

Graceful, attractive, calm, Dr. Yvonne Wolfe fit the job description. She seemed content with herself, yet empathetic to my concerns. She'd obtained her PhD while raising two girls, and still spoke with affection about her husband. Her clothes embodied comfort and style in the same outfit, with hair neatly sculpted but not helmetized with hairspray as so often happens with women beyond the age of sixty in Dallas. I settled into the couch in her office.

"Tell me about yourself." Dr. Yvonne leaned back in her black leather chair.

We went through the basics and ended up talking about Dad and Mom.

Dad: Career Naval officer. Hardworking. Loved by all. From a family of thirteen children in a Polish lower-income neighborhood in Detroit. Favorite slogan: "If you can't say anything nice . . ." Brilliant athlete. Incredible physique. Wore checkered shorts and black socks on the country club tennis court. Liked to garden and cook. Had a hug that swallowed me, made me feel safe. He retired to become a finance professor. Died of cancer at age fifty-eight.

Mom: Bright. Often frustrated with her role as a mother. Screamer. Funny. Sarcastic. Sharp dresser. She liked martinis with olives, lots of them. Later, rum manhattans became her drink. Later, she switched to vodka. More than once, after happy hour, she played Broadway show tunes and got us to march to John Philip Sousa. At fifty-one, Mom got her master's degree in counseling and worked for the state mental hospital, specializing in addictions. Mom had a knack for order. The people she counseled might have scattered lives due to alcohol or drugs, but Mom pounded structure back into their days. Mom is tiny, barely five feet tall, but she can take down anyone in less than a sentence. Mom started her own counseling practice at age sixty-five. When most people dream of retirement, she was just opening shop.

Dr. Yvonne listened as I laid out my family history over several sessions. She wanted to understand my family of origin, and with that information, help me understand why I react the way I do with my husband, my children, and the world around me.

My genetic predisposition for depression showed in most branches of my family tree, expressed in different ways. Dr. Yvonne wanted to understand what set off my genetic tendency for bleakness. And once I understood those triggers, Dr. Yvonne explained, I could manage my depression more effectively. A person can be prone to heart disease, but she can avoid early onset of the disease through proper diet, exercise, and stress reduction. I needed to understand my emotional equivalent to french fries.

Dr. Yvonne asked me to describe my family dinner table, a situation with conflict—perhaps that might offer some clues.

"Did you talk at the table? Was anyone the de facto winner? Can you describe one night?"

I sank back into the couch and tried to remember. We weren't the Cleavers.

I drew a blank. I asked Dr. Yvonne if I could think about it, then write about my family. Dr. Yvonne agreed writing might help me dissect my family's tendencies.

She glanced at her watch. "Look at that, we're out of time."

The psychotherapy clock ticks despite the content or movement of the discussion. That day the session cooperated with the clock, but there were other days when I felt cut off, the hour ending before a revelation fully hatched. Other days, talking seemed a step above babble. I understood, from the beginning, that Dr. Yvonne was a guide. She had a stake in my recovery; she'd help me, but if I wanted to stay well, I had to focus on the why of my depression outside of our sessions. Insight does not reveal itself in neatly packaged, hourly increments. Deciphering my life was my responsibility.

Armed with Dr. Yvonne's challenge, I hopped in my car, the chairs to my childhood dinner table scraping the floor as they settled to their spots in my brain.

6

My Childhood Family Table

Strawberries and whipped cream with that?" I eyed the angel food cake on the counter.

Mom shook her head no. "Penuche." She sipped her rum manhattan while she stirred the concoction.

My mouth watered with thoughts of brown sugar and butter. I'd made a penuche topping before, stirred the bubbling syrup until it thickened. She poured the mixture over the top of the cake. The glaze dribbled down the sides.

"Almost forgot. Condiments." Mom nodded toward four blue ceramic bowls, each one smaller than a teacup, and instructed me to fill them with crushed peanuts, coconut, chutney, and raisins. "Be careful." Mom watched as I cradled one bowl in my two hands.

"What's this stuff for?" The bowl of coconut, held like a chalice, balanced on my fingertips.

"To sprinkle on the shrimp curry. It's an Indian dish, from India—not from Cowboys and Indians."

At the age of eight, I wasn't sure I understood the difference.

Mom sighed and looked at her watch.

"Where *is* your father?" The way her voice raised on "is," Mom made a comment, not a question. She said this most nights as the clock ticked past 6:30 p.m., as though she expected him to arrive at 5:00 p.m., even though he never did.

Wheels crunched in the driveway. A car door slammed.

"Finally." Mom cut the green pepper into thin strips.

Dad opened the side door into the kitchen, as I pulled the knob. He clutched a wide black notebook under his left arm and a manila folder in his right, both overflowing with papers.

"Hey, hon," he nodded to Mom. "It's nasty out there. Got the news on?" He set his notebook on one of the three rattan barstools that lined the counter, hung his coat in the closet outside the kitchen, pulled a chair from the kitchen table, and sat on the edge of his seat in front of the TV.

"How about 'How was your day?'" Mom said.

"That beltway, it's unbelievable!" Dad's eyes focused on the black and white screen.

"My day—" Mom threw the peppers into the salad.

Dad leaned closer to the TV. A woman with long, dark hair outstretched her arms above her head in what seemed a challenge, not surrender, to the policemen who surrounded her.

"Joe?"

"Crazy, that's what this is . . . ," Dad pointed at the TV. "Folk singers blocking draftees. Joan Baez—what the hell does she know? She's probably an agent for the Viet Cong."

"What's Viet Cong?" I edged closer. Mom took off her apron and took a long sip from her rum manhattan. She handed Dad a glass.

"Thanks, dear. Dinner smells great."

"Hello would be nice," she said as she ruffled his hair. Dad grabbed my mother around the waist and nuzzled her hip.

"What's Viet Cong?" I repeated.

"An evil group," he muttered. "Communists."

Mom pushed his arm away.

"Come on, Joe," Mom placed her hands on my shoulders and directed me away from Dad. "It's a little more complicated than that, don't you think?"

"If you look—" Dad talked with his eyes fixed on the TV.

"It's time for dinner. Julie, can you call everyone?"

"What's a Communist?" I reached back and put my hand on Dad's shoulder.

"Julie!" Mom's tone got my attention, so I rounded up my siblings.

After Patrick, Matt, Eileen, and Teddy joined us, I asked again. "What's a Communist?"

"Oh God, here we go again." Patrick pulled out his chair. Home on break from Duke University, Patrick had just refused an ROTC scholarship.

"Joe." Mom pointed toward the TV. "Turn that off. Dinner's ready."

"Just a second . . . ," Dad brushed her back with his left hand. "I want to see this."

Eileen rested her hand on the back of Dad's chair.

"Dad," Eileen dragged her words with teenage impatience. "You're in my seat."

"What's a Communist?" I whispered from my place at the table.

"All right, all right, all right!" Dad stood up, turned off the TV, and took his seat at the head of the table. Mom moved to her chair, opposite his. I always sat on Dad's right, a dangerous spot. Dad kept a large wooden spoon at the table for etiquette enforcement. If I leaned my elbows on the table during the course of a meal, Dad taught his lesson with a firm whack on my arm. Dad didn't pick on me, but being on the right hand of the father left me at a distinct disadvantage. The older siblings filed into place, my younger brother Teddy next to me. We put our napkins in our laps.

Dad began, and we all joined in.

"Bless us, Oh Lord, and these Thy gifts, which we are about to receive from Thy bounty, through Christ, Our Lord. Amen."

We passed the bowl filled with steaming white rice, then the shrimp curry, each forming our own pile on our plates. Dad cleared his throat when I ladled a second heaping spoonful of rice on mine.

"Try a little salad," he said.

"What's a Communist, Dad?" I held the bowl for Teddy as he spooned his rice.

"Someone who steals freedom. Someone who wants everyone to be the same."

Teddy passed the bowl to Mom. He took his fork in his left hand and gulped a bite down. He clenched the knife in his right hand.

"Gee, Dad, I thought you'd like that," Patrick smirked. "Share it all." He sprinkled peanuts on his mound of shrimp curry with the tiny spoon. "Sounds pretty Christian."

Mom dropped her fork on her plate and leaned forward, left fist on her hip, right elbow bent, bobbing a pointed finger at Patrick.

"Look, you who dropped his ROTC scholarship because you couldn't get a date with short hair. Don't make fun of your father. How are we going to pay—"

"My hair?" Patrick stabbed a shrimp with his fork. "Is that what you think this is about? Hair?" He popped the shrimp into his mouth and chewed. "I'll find a job, take out loans, but there's no way I'm fighting in that war."

Teddy cleared his throat and set his utensils down. I crunched the peanuts between my teeth. The sweetness of the raisins lingered, mixed with the salt. I mixed the bright yellow curry into the white rice.

"Pat," Dad said, "if you're called to serve your country, you must—"

"Serve my country, my ass! Nobody asked me for a vote on Vietnam. Nobody asked Vietnam about Vietnam."

I took a bite of food. I looked at Dad, then Patrick, then Dad, then back, my fork on autopilot, shoveling rice. I didn't want to miss anything, a night at the fights.

Dad raised his right forearm, fingers straight, thumb curled, karate chop style. "If you'll look at the facts . . ." Dad chopped the air as he spoke, emphasizing four words. *Look at the facts.* ChopChopChopChop. His hand froze on *facts* to drive the point home. When Dad used this phrase, as he often did, I knew he was right. Dad was infallible, like the Pope, but better.

Patrick leapt into Dad's dramatic pause. "The *fact* is the US marched into Vietnam and proclaimed our country God's gift to government. LBJ was a fascist. Nixon is a fascist—"

"Okay, Patrick, let's have the Viet Cong run our schools," Dad said calmly, his voice mismatched with his words. "Then you'll have a lot of choices. Maybe they can stick bamboo shoots up your fingernails—"

44

"You're a fascist. Brainwashed!" Patrick pointed his finger in Dad's face.

"Maybe they can cut your future child from your wife's womb." The words formed in the back of my Dad's throat, condensed, professorial, as though he trapped his squirming anger in his chest. He gripped his wooden spoon. I shrank back, ensuring my elbows were nowhere near the table.

"Joe! The little kids . . . What's wrong with you?" Mom looked at Dad, while Teddy and I looked at each other. Dad looked at the wooden spoon, surprised, as if he didn't know how it got there. He set the spoon down, ran his fingers on top of it, as if to make sure the spoon stayed in place.

"What's a womb?" Teddy asked.

"Propaganda!" Patrick's volume increased as his words expanded. "Can't you see? They squelch anyone who opposes them. Look at Joan Baez—"

"Let's look at Joan Baez," Dad said. "Protesting is fine, she can make a sign or sing her ballads." His eyes moved from Patrick to Eileen, hoping he might find an ally. "Baez is blocking the entrance to a building. Impeding the process. Joan Kumbaya Baez doesn't get that."

Eileen slammed her glass on the table. She looked away. Second eldest, she'd heard a lot of these speeches.

"The process toward death, Dad," Patrick said. "Don't you get that?"

Matt grabbed the rice, piled it high on his plate—bulking up for football. Matt had a strategic approach to family interaction, just like he did with sports. If you can't win, disengage. Find another route. Play smarter. At his small size, he'd learned on the field, the hard way.

"People are dying, Joe," Mom said, her pitch rising. "Kids. Children. Not much older than ours."

We all stopped, listened for the next word.

Silence didn't happen often at our table. With seven people, sound was ever present. Forks and knives on plates, chairs thudding against linoleum, voices colliding, laughter, swallows, grunts—even when the words stopped, the noises didn't. I could hear the wind, a steady breeze, through the glass behind me. But the silence only lasted a second.

"Let's see," Dad ticked the items off on his fingers. "Would you rather have your churches bombed? Be forced from your home in a skiff? Have your civilian officials murdered along with their wives, children, and the family cat?" He paused for an answer, but no one responded. I moved my rice from one side of the plate to the other. "That's what communism buys you."

Patrick pushed his chair away from the table.

"How can you be so sure?" Mom asked.

"It's the facts," Dad said. "Documented."

"But our kids? Should our kids *die* for them?"

Eileen took another sip. Teddy scooted closer to me. Our legs touched beneath the table.

"If need be," Dad said.

"If need be? What kind of answer is that?"

"What? It's fine for them to suffer but not us? We're not obliged to help?" Dad shrugged. "Let's sit back then." He leaned back in his chair and flung his arms to his sides for emphasis. "Let's do nothing."

"I didn't say—"

Dad leaned forward. "Just don't complain when communism knocks on your door."

Mom and Dad were quiet for a moment. I could feel something rumbling in the air although no one said anything, like water ready to boil.

"Don't you *feel* anything?" Mom delivered her words in staccato, like darts. "What if Patrick gets drafted? Killed? Will that hurt you? 'If need be.' What are you? Spock, our Vulcan leader? Run the odds for success and take the gamble?"

Teddy shimmied back in his seat, and I leaned forward. Matt rolled his eyes, and Eileen squirmed in her chair as if she wanted to leave but couldn't.

"Can I be excused?" Patrick scooted his chair back. "I'm meeting some friends."

Excused? But what about the cake? The icing? I never missed dessert. "Paddy, we still have—"

"Just look at the facts," Dad's priority wasn't cake.

"Facts? Fine, Mr. Spock." Mom shook her finger at him across the table. "Don't make me have these babies and then kill them with your facts, okay?"

"Get a hold of yourself, I know down deep we agree on this."

"Deep down . . ." Mom looked into her cocktail glass. The liquid gone, she swirled the ice.

"Mom," I whispered, "what about the angel food cake?" Mom eyed the Ron Rico on the counter and sucked an ice cube in her mouth. Her jaw flexed as she crunched it and swallowed.

"Maybe I'll make myself another half," she said.

"Mom?"

She got up from her seat, empty dish and glass in her hands. She moved around the counter to the sink, which faced the kitchen table. When she dropped the plastic dish in the sink, the plate clattered.

"Julie?" Mom set the glass on the plate, her eyes focused on the task. "Will you help me serve the cake?"

7

Beyond Teacup Fiction

*W*riting helps you." Dr. Yvonne took another sip of tea. We discussed my dinner table story. "Write some more. Give yourself an excuse to be alone."

"But I'm a mom, a wife. I don't have time to be alone."

"You need to make time," she said. "You're drawn to chaos, to diversity, to a collision of thought, but there's a side of you that needs solitude."

Solitude. The sound of the word made me switch gears. Something in her voice calmed me, made me realize that we wouldn't find the answer to depression in a few sessions. I knew she was right, but I wasn't a monk. How was I going to squeeze solitude into my life?

I imagined different scenarios, along with Ken's questions at the end of the day. Did you buy clothes for the kids? Did you print the soccer schedule? What about dinner? *No dear, I needed my solitude.*

"When? How can I spend that much time on myself?"

"Sign up for a writing class. Give yourself some deadlines." Dr. Yvonne shook her head. "Spend time with yourself or be spent. Your choice."

A few days later, when I thought about cramming solitude between yoga, art class, and an epic nonfiction work on depression, I received a sign. Signs are coincidences so closely linked that I'm convinced of

49

divine intervention. A friend handed me a flier. "I heard you were trying to write a book."

The black letters leapt from the flier. Writing group. No degree required. Informal setting. Professional advice in a relaxed environment.

I made the call.

Eden, the writing group instructor, clustered words into slingshot sentences aimed to make a point. Her out-of-state roots showed long before she mentioned "Chicahhgo." Surrounded by soft Texas drawls for so long, I'd forgotten some women—like Eden—had voices with an edge.

Eden explained the format for the class. The group met in her home. Each week Eden assigned a piece of literature to review the first half of class, then in the second half, we'd critique a story written by one of the group members, all aspiring writers. By the end of the phone call, I'd committed to the class.

The assignments for the first class arrived via mail late one afternoon. I ripped open the envelope. The kids were hungry, badgering me about dinner.

"Have a cheese stick." I walked into my office, shut the door, and began to read.

Ray Bradbury's *How to Keep and Feed a Muse* ignited my thoughts. Muse. I hadn't heard that word for years. Since having kids, my reading shrank into snippets of time, like commercial breaks or sound bites. I read in carpool, that fifteen minutes squeezed in before Ken got home from work, and usually a few pages before I slumped into bed. Bradbury felt like a lifeline.

I moved to the next assignment—a Stuart Dybek story. I sped through until I read, "She was dressed like a clarinet, reedy thin in a black dress with silver buttons, a silver belt, and a matching necklace." I underlined the sentence in bright blue ink and wrote my assessment in the margin. *Wow.* I felt the pull of something in my chest. *Could I write a sentence like that?*

I heard the garage door. Shit. It was 7 p.m. Ken's footsteps sounded in the hallway outside my office. He paused. Without a knock, he pushed the door open and walked next to my chair. His briefcase hung on his shoulder.

"Why's the door closed?" He plopped his briefcase on my desk and planted a kiss on my lips.

"Ah . . ."

"What's for dinner?"

I shuffled the papers on my desk. Ken turned, walked out of my office, and looked around. He stepped back in.

"Where are the kids?"

Where were the kids? They'd been quiet, or at least I thought they'd been quiet. Hell, a bomb could've exploded outside my door. The muffled sounds from the movie room saved me.

"Oh, they're watching TV." I jumped up from my seat and threw my arms around him.

"Geez," he grinned. "What happened today?"

"Lots, this stuff, this class, you know what Bradbury says—"

"Whoa, girl, I want to hear. Really. But let's eat first."

The doors from the movie room opened, and the kids emerged as if on cue.

"When's dinner?" Becka asked. "I'm hungry."

My eyes moved from Andrew, to Becka, to Ken. *Solitude? Who am I kidding?*

Ken lifted his briefcase strap to his shoulder.

"Let me drop this on my desk." He moved toward the door and called back, "How about Boston Market?"

The first class built my confidence and sparked more ideas. Despite advanced educations, no one had published anything in the general market. Eden talked about plot, said things like, "Fiction drapes the story in a vehicle that moves through time."

I rediscovered the world with a keen writer's eye. Ordinary objects took on metaphoric meaning. During my early morning run, I smelled hyacinth, worshipped the moon, and adopted a practice I'd kept as a small child. Look at a house, see the front door, and imagine. Who lives there? Who is the father, the mother, or is there one? Who is that boy with the deep scowl? What happens?

I envisioned my books, written and published, spread on Oprah's coffee table.

"What was it," Oprah would ask, "that started your brilliant career at forty-one?"

"Well," I imagined my response, confident but with great humility, "it all started with a sign, a mere piece of paper." These fantasies played in my head, each one better than the one before. By the following week, I was ready, sure to be the next Great American Novelist.

"Let's begin with Julie's story," Eden said.

My story described a trip with Ken to Lourdes. Metaphorically, the story addressed my depression. Would anyone catch the deeper meaning?

We sat in a circle, six women, me the youngest; most of the others were five to ten years older than me. Everyone dressed better than I did, but that didn't take too much effort. I wore jeans and Tevas. My toenails were polished.

"Chandani," Eden nodded, "you've done this before. You start." Chandani had a PhD in English literature.

"This is a start, a good start," Chandani's soft voice enunciated words with precision. "But you need more physical description of the main character." She went on. "You also change tenses here—you jump from past to present tense."

I glanced at the paper. She was absolutely right. *How did I miss that?*

We moved to Pam, a woman from the affluent Highland Park area. She appeared neatly pressed—blouse matched pants, pants matched shoes, eye shadow coordinated to bring out her blue eyes. Every part of her seemed tastefully done, without a wrinkle. I prepared to dislike whatever she said before she spoke.

"I love the scene where you and Ken are in the crowd. You know, with those people on stretchers waiting to be healed?" Pam laughed. "Then the Italian lady yaps on the phone, in the middle of 'Ave Maria.'" Pam straightened her blouse. "Did she really do that?"

"Yes, it's true—"

"Julie," Eden interrupted, "no comments until the end. And Pam, when we critique, remember never to address the main character as 'you.' This is not about Julie; the story is about the main character."

Pam and I glanced at each other. "Thanks," I mouthed. Pam nodded.

Joanne, the artist, weighed in next. "It's descriptive, but I feel the narrator is keeping the reader at arm's length. I want inside the narrator's head."

Inside my head? How do I get that on paper? I wanted to ask, but waited for my turn.

We continued around the room, each person offering impressions. Everyone seemed hesitant to say anything critical. Some liked this line or that description, and I basked in the compliments. There weren't as many as I anticipated, but I still felt good.

We rounded the circle to Eden. She took my story, pulled out her glasses, and examined her notes. She set my story down. She shook her head, as if she had a chill, then zeroed in on me.

"Your story feels like spit-up from an infant; you know, that stuff with lumps in it."

Spit up? I felt like she'd spewed on me.

I said nothing. That was the rule. The writer couldn't comment until everyone finished the first round of critiques. I studied the cross in my Tevas, the chips in my polish.

Eden pointed to the page. "You're hiding something here."

Did she see through me? Was my depression that transparent?

"At the end, something happened, but what?" In the second half of the story, I run until I reach a hill that overlooks Lourdes. I am overwhelmed. I cry, knowing in my mind that I live only because my suicide attempt failed. That admission never reached the page. Instead, in the story, I cry and thank God for life.

Eden looked at me, hawk-like, talons extended. Her dark hair, thick and wild about her face, fell into her eyes. She pushed a strand back.

"Crying? Giving thanks to God? I don't get it. As a writer, you need to distance yourself. This may have happened to you, but to write well, you need to think of yourself as a character in a story. Build the emotion. What happened to the character? What's a reasonable reaction?" Eden paused. "There's got to be more."

I glanced down, unable to lift my chin. I saw only knees. Some legs crossed, some not. *A reasonable reaction?* Depression always seems an overwrought response to everyone except to the person lost in the perspective depression creates. *How do I explain this to them? To anyone?* We sat in Eden's den, a small, comfortable space, with books stacked floor to ceiling. Her fat gray Persian twisted around her legs.

I sighed. "There . . . there is more."

"So what is it? Lay it out there."

Lay it out there? That I'd tried to kill myself? How could I tell my story when I didn't understand it myself? Eden had no idea she was playing with dynamite. How would these women react to a locked psychiatric ward? I imagined the shock on their faces. ECT. Cuckoo's Nest. Official member. *Can they accept what I have done?*

"Are you there?" Eden persisted. "Come on, how bad can it be? Give us some substance!" She shook her head. "Otherwise, this is a step above teacup fiction."

"Teacup?"

"You know, trite, bullshit stuff. I don't have time for writers like that."

Teacup? I lifted my head, moved from face to face. *Bullshit?* I could feel the heat rise from my lower back, past my shoulders, and lodge in my neck. *Trite?* This was my life. This was me, not some character, not some fiction I played with to entertain myself.

I had to tell them. Without metaphors, without a scenic backdrop, I had to be honest. They needed plain, undecorated clarity. Otherwise, my writing was bullshit, wasting their time and mine.

I felt an admission at my lips. I'd be naked. *Can I risk this? Will they judge me?* Something inside me exploded. I heard the words as if someone else spoke them. "I was in a locked psychiatric ward." My face flushed. No one gasped, but the room sucked in a collective breath.

"Okay," Eden sounded approachable for the first time. "That's a worthy topic. Can you talk about it? Do you want to talk about it?"

The tears streamed down my face. "I was depressed," I said between gulps. "Had to, had to do . . . How can I tell you this?"

54

"What? Medication?" Eden shrugged. "That's no news. Bet half the women in this room are on something."

Pam and Sandy, the two women from Highland Park, exchanged glances, as if they might be the next ones outed.

"ECT. Shock therapy."

"Holy shit." Eden looked at me in disbelief. What was this live science experiment on display in her house? "I didn't think they did that anymore." She stood up, reached over to the tissue box on the bookcase. She handed me a tissue.

I nodded, blew my nose. "ECT saved my life."

"Okay." Eden resumed her seat. "This is enough for today." She stared at me, brown eyes intense. "You need to write about this."

"What? How . . . how do I start?"

"It doesn't matter. Write about something that means something, something you know. Block some hours on your calendar and write."

Class over, we poured out the door, each person headed to her separate car. The other women fastened their seatbelts, waved good-bye and mouthed, "Nice to meet you," as they drove off. I waved back, mouthed the same words, but didn't start my car. We were civilized, our emotions repackaged, fastened in for the ride home. Within minutes, no one was left on the street.

Solitude.

I pulled out my Palm Pilot and found a few hourlong blocks in the following week. I tapped in the words—writing time. Finished, I turned the keys in the ignition. The daffodils in a neighbor's yard caught my eye, brilliant, yellow. I rolled down the windows, breathing in the crisp spring air.

8

Buried Pain

*B*ored with the tire swing, I plunged deep into the woods. The forest smelled of wet earth. Fallen trees rotted, and orange mushrooms sprouted. Spider webs hung from limbs, strands outlined with beads of moisture. A cardinal called his mate, and red darted after brown across, up, down, until the two settled on a branch. A stream of light cut from the forest ceiling to the ground. Flecks of dust spiraled in a pure beam. The light lingered, then shifted and disappeared.

When I exited a thicket of trees near my house, I found my mother on the back porch. A broom in hand, she hummed while she worked. I traversed the lawn, silent. I put my hand on the door, hoping to sneak by without an assignment.

Mom glanced up. "Don't go in there! You're a mess, covered in mud—" Mom's version of outdoors was a barbeque and a manicured lawn. She shook her head. "We need to get you some new clothes; you look like a ragamuffin."

I brushed the dirt from my shorts. Mom loved to shop, especially for clothes. I lacked the shopping gene. Mom swooned over patent leather for a childhood shoe; I liked bare feet. Compromise often proved difficult.

Mom flicked a leaf from the cement. "What'd you see today, Miss Annie Oakley?"

I thought for a moment, then answered the obvious. "God."

"What?" She set the broom aside. "You had a vision?" A good Catholic, Mom knew the stories of Bernadette and Fatima.

"No, just God." I stuck my hands in my pockets and found a rock from an earlier exploration. I told Mom about the light, my holy incident in the woods.

She laughed, bent to her knees, picked a twig out of my hair. "That's just light, silly, not God."

I didn't argue. I knew the light was God, even if my mother didn't.

Some of my best memories of early childhood are from two places—the woods or my bedroom closet. I never found solitude lonely. Maybe because I moved six times before my seventh birthday, I didn't play the games American girls typically play. Dolls, Barbies, or dress-up didn't rank with my journal, a crayfish hunt, or a God-sighting in the woods. The forest gave my ideas clarity, something I lost when surrounded by others.

In my Annandale house, I wrote in my closet, a bare bulb glowing above my head. Huddled on the wooden floor, my notebook balanced on my knees, journal entries and poems tumbled out of my pencil. Topics ranged from toys and cats to Jesus and generation gaps.

My room was the smallest, with pale yellow walls and orange curtains fringed with brown fuzzy balls and held back with a sash. Only inches separated my bed and a few pieces of white furniture with a flowing gold trim. The walls felt close but not tight, a safe womb for my ideas. My one window overlooked cherry trees, bushes, and bulbs, all planted by my dad. By late April, our front yard exploded in a sea of pink and yellow. On more than one night, I stood on tiptoe, pushed the window open, and surveyed the world from my safe perch.

At ten, I moved from my yellow room into my sister's blue room. Mom needed an office, a place to write her master's thesis. Mom wanted a room of her own, so she took mine. I didn't protest the move. My sister, Eileen, was away at college. I'd only have to share the bigger, better blue room with her on holidays. We all viewed the move to the blue room as a move up.

Mom's career in counseling emerged after her own long bout of depression. Mom told me later she never contemplated suicide; five kids, numerous moves, and piles of laundry never afforded that much time to think. Besides, Mom preferred verbal assault to self-flagellation. She screamed, cleaned, and worried about germs, money, and sins I never saw her commit. On some Saturday mornings, she woke me with a vacuum under my bed. She attacked dirt with an intensity only matched by her dread of pinworms.

Dad took the brunt of Mom's anger. In her forties, Mom lived most days resenting her life. Mom blamed Dad for her unhappy state, then the Church, then after three years with her psychiatrist, herself. She didn't want five kids, she told me once. Three was plenty. Being the fourth, I was stung by the news.

Motherhood and shifts in geography eclipsed my mother in a way that no new hair color, outfit, or cocktail could escape. Twice a week, she'd lie down on the couch and list her problems as Dr. Jamison sat behind her head and unraveled her thoughts. "He could only see my feet," she told me, "so I made sure I wore my best shoes."

Some people become born-again Christians. My mother became a born-again psychologist. Spurred by her new religion, Mom began an expedition of self-discovery. Parapsychology, reflexology, reading auras, mind control, mantras, astrology, tarot cards, and palm reading. In the folk group at church, Mom belted songs while she cheered the changes of Vatican II. I couldn't bite into a piece of toast at breakfast without her wondering aloud, "What do you mean?"

Mom settled on a short, frosted hairstyle that gave her a flash of elegance and didn't worry about her extra fifteen pounds. During our trip to France, she ordered "café glace" with a broad smile and a wave of her hand.

Dad applauded her pursuits. He loved *her*, not some stagnant image in his head. Mom returned Dad's love but measured her affection. She gave only so much, always careful to preserve herself.

Mom wrote her thesis in my yellow room, while I lived in Eileen's blue room. The rug, the walls, even the pattern on the curtains sported a pale blue. A *blue* blue—not a bright blue or electric blue or anything with intensity. That nearly transparent blue sucked my energy. The closet, shallow and wide, lacked the depth for a writing perch.

When Eileen returned home on breaks from college, we shared the blue room. Besides the challenges a seven-year age gap might bring, I was a slob. My version of cleaning up consisted of piling items in the closet. I forced the door closed.

I slept on the top bunk. Late one afternoon, I curled up in my bed with my journal. The door flew open. Eileen tripped over my pile of clothes.

"Julie!" She threw my clothes on the top bunk.

I peaked over the edge. "Sorry." I sat up, wadded the clothes in a ball.

Eileen had a towel wrapped around her body and another around her wet hair. Late Friday afternoon, she had little time to get ready for her date. With peak efficiency, she pulled on underwear, bra, jeans, shirt, and belt. She applied mascara, blush, and picked out a necklace. She turned to the closet to find her shoes. A wave of panic hit me. I had just cleaned up.

Eileen pulled open the sliding door to find a pile of clothes, books, and a tree branch piled in the closet. The door jammed, stuck on some unseen item.

"Julie!"

I scrambled down the bunk and knocked my journal off the bed. Eileen picked up the journal.

"Give that back!" I tumbled to the floor.

Eileen scanned through pages. I wondered if she saw my latest poem. I'd written many patriotic poems and read them over the loudspeaker at school. She slammed the book shut and handed it back to me. "Do you put anything away? How can you live like this?"

"Did you like my poem?

"What poem? I'm looking for my shoes!"

I opened my journal to the poem. "Here," I read aloud in an authoritative voice. "America. There is a country I am told, A country fierce, a country bold."

Eileen looked at me, dumbfounded. "Ever hear of the draft?"

"No, but Dad says—"

She shook her head. "Never mind—you'll never get it." She turned to the closet and burrowed for her shoes. She found one. She put the shoe on her foot and continued to search. ·

Eileen pulled at something that rattled the closet door. "Damn it!"

I inched toward the bedroom door to make my escape.

"My shoe's stuck in the door!"

I could hear her voice as I ran down the stairs.

"You're such a slob! You're going to pay for this . . ."

I sprinted out the sliding glass doors, across the backyard, and into the woods, to an oak tree discovered on an earlier walk. I felt drawn to this tree. Eileen's anger rattled in my head. I missed my yellow room, missed having my own space. Whatever I did, I seemed in the way, a nuisance.

I placed my hand on the jagged bark. A squirrel approached, snatched an acorn, and bolted. With my head against the tree, I stretched out, the leaves my mattress. I looked up at the intersecting limbs. The light penetrated in clear, short bursts. The trees swayed in the wind, started a flickering sun dance. My thoughts lifted to the top branches and scattered in the sky.

Along with the blue room came an introduction to junior high, passion, and unrequited love. I was trapped in a body that sprouted breasts and grew hairs in odd places with gorilla-like legs hidden under fuzzy kneesocks. My continuous one eyebrow topped a glaring smile of silver braces strung together by rubber bands.

My friend Patti Weinberg couldn't believe that I could reach eleven years and know as little as I did. She assumed full responsibility for my education. She dragged me to the girls' room to teach me the basics—Bobby Sherman's eye color, the Partridge Family's best song, and what really happened on Dark Shadows, a show my mother never let me watch.

Then, in segments and intervals, she taught me to cuss.

I don't know why Patti thought a foul mouth might help my image, but she maintained the mission. We started with the easy words—"shit, bitch, damn, hell"—and worked our way to "fuck."

Patti would say a word, provide a definition, and then use the expletive to make sure I understood. Sort of like Spanish class. *Escucha y repetirse.* We became so brazen in our training program that we passed notes during class. "Miss Carr is a bitch." "Tom is a conceited little shit." Miss Carr intercepted our note exchange right as I sacrificed my friend Connie on the page. "Connie fucks herself." What did Connie do to deserve that? I didn't think about Connie. For me, the word held secret powers. My pencil scratched the letters as the blood of adventure pulsed in my veins, right up to the moment Miss Carr's pale white hand snatched the note in midair.

Miss Carr gave me the option to tell my parents myself or let her tell them. I hung my head and told my mom. Mom called me a gutter mouth and sent me to my room. When Dad got home, he knocked on my door. Dad sat down on the bed where I cried into my pillow.

"Heard about the note."

"Yeah." The pillow muffled my voice.

"Do you know what the word means?"

"Sure, Dad." I wanted to shock him. "I know what fuck means." I glared at him, ready for a fight.

He shook his head and smiled.

I didn't understand what he found so funny. My teeth defied the braces and ground together.

Dad took a deep breath. "Julie, that word . . ." He looked at his hands.

"What about it?"

"Guys on the ship used it all the time. The word doesn't surprise me. It just . . ."

I put my face back in the pillow.

"Misses the point." He touched my shoulder, but I inched away. "Sex is more than bodies, it's . . . connection. Sex is the most a loving couple can give each other."

I turned my head but wouldn't look at him.

"*Fuck* steals that," he said. "Don't you see? When you use that word, you hope that connection never happens. Does that make sense?"

Dad's lessons on sex seemed crafted from the fairytales my mother read to me. I wanted to believe him. I wanted to be that pure. My

Dad's cotton shirt caught my tears but couldn't stop them. He gave me a long, firm hug. Most of the time, Dad didn't talk much. Sometimes he made his best points without speaking.

About the time my braces came off and I plucked one eyebrow into two, the blue room became a place to drop at night and nothing more. I didn't change the color. My relationship with Eileen improved in those years, but she came back from college in strange forms I couldn't understand. One time she weighed a hundred pounds and had an answer for any question asked. The next time she was fifty pounds heavier, a 50 percent increase on her petite five-feet-two-inch frame. She lay in bed for hours, something she never did in her worst moods while living with me. She didn't seem like the same person.

All my Mom's courses in counseling suggested therapy and tough love for depression. They hired a counselor, monitored her eating and sleeping, and prayed. In the 1970s, doctors didn't prescribe antidepressants like Tic Tacs.

My parents, trying to impose structure on Eileen's lethargic days, pushed her to work. Eileen waited tables, not the best occupation for a depressed person. She looked miserable. "Cancel, cancel," my mother reminded her with a pointed finger. "No negative thoughts." Good thing we never kept a gun in the house.

I didn't show any overt signs of depression until my freshman year of college. One pattern of behavior, however, was set long before that age. When hurt, I accelerated and buried pain.

A friend can slow or stop that cycle. Pain shared with a friend dissipates pain. Once I reached adolescence, trees alone no longer soothed my angst. I needed a friend, a best friend.

My friendship with Karen, initiated in sixth grade, served exactly that purpose. We pounded the way to each other's houses, one mile linked by suburban sidewalk. We talked for hours, about boys, about girls, about our parents, sometimes sneaking a cigarette. When dinner neared, we walked back to our houses. We called each other on the phone after we ate.

In April of my seventh-grade year, Karen moved to California for a year. I was devastated. I cried, she cried. I wrote her a poem that ended "Cause what is tomorrow without my best friend?" Our parents thought us hormone-charged, overly dramatic adolescents.

I packed in activities—cheerleading, schoolwork, Young Life, acting, directing. Unsatisfied with a mere participant role, I led everything I tried. Friends and family told me I did too much, but I didn't listen.

I sped up because I couldn't stand the silence, something I once sought for comfort. The pace worked like a sedative with its own addictive allure. With no time to think, the hurt faded. When Karen returned a year later, my pace never slowed. The pace had become my friend, my elixir. I no longer needed a confidant.

A jet-propelled life eventually takes a physical toll. I contracted pneumonia in the fall of my sophomore year of high school. I ignored the cough for two months, unable to miss any practice, game, or rehearsal. Mom finally dragged me to Bethesda Naval Hospital. They sent me back, declaring me healthy. I sneered, "I told you," in my mother's face. A week later I couldn't breathe.

During the second visit to Bethesda, the doctor told me I'd have to be hospitalized.

"I can't." I shook my head at the impossibility. "I have a game on Saturday, the play Saturday night, there's no way I—"

"Look," he interrupted, "one lung is completely filled. The other is half-full. Your choice is to stay in the hospital or die in two weeks."

As much as I might've believed in spiritual healing, I didn't want to take that gamble. My mom checked me into the hospital and left.

For some reason, my parents couldn't stay with me at the hospital. Being one of five children, I didn't question this or even feel bad about this situation; it just was. My doctor entered the room where I waited. His dark-rimmed glasses, pale skin, and trace of acne around the corners of his temples hinted that most of his college years were spent with books, not people, and definitely not women. He told me in monotone that because I had a cough for a number of weeks, he'd do a test for cancer. *Cancer! First dying in two weeks, now cancer, what next?* He pushed the rim of his glasses up to the far arc of his nose.

"We'll have to do a Pap smear. Do you know what that is?"

I didn't. I was fifteen. I shook my head blankly. "No."

"You're not a virgin, right?"

My mouth hung open as I tried to understand the connection between coughs, cancers, Pap smears, and virginity. I squinted.

"Well, . . ." he waited, the arms of his white coat crossed over his stethoscope.

"Yes," I stammered. "I'm a virgin."

"Oh, come on," he smirked. "You've got to be kidding. You're no virgin."

"But I am!"

"Yeah, right." He took off his glasses and wiped the lens with the end of his white coat. "Okay, virgin girl, I've got you scheduled for a Pap smear later this afternoon."

I didn't know what to expect, but when the nurse told me to lie back on the pad, spread my legs, and put my feet in those silver stirrups, I knew it couldn't be good. I pushed down the sides of my paper gown to cover my skin. The doctor's shoes scraped when he entered. He walked between the stirrups and pressed my left leg aside. "Hmm," he grunted and then turned on his heel and left the room.

God, I hope he's not doing anything else.

He returned two minutes later with ten other people. Ten. I squished my knees together and pulled the paper gown taut. He pried my knees apart and lifted the gown as though I were a cadaver. I closed my eyes.

"This, my friends, is a virgin. Take a close look because you won't get a chance to see many of these."

I didn't cry. Something shut down, detached as the interns whispered and my doctor paraded my body like a freak at the circus sideshow. My brain went to work. I watched my body encased in a transparent shield, a bullet-proof glass box, from a safe corner of the ceiling. The shield was cold, metallic, like the steel probe he carelessly thrust into my vagina. He scraped my cervix for a sample.

"That's it." He dropped his gloves in the trash.

I felt the shield falter and my mind slip back into my body. I opened my eyes as he leaned his face close to my ear, whispering so no one else could hear, "I guess now you know what it feels like."

The words hung in the air. I turned my head away from him and felt blood drip from my body to the paper sheet beneath me. The interns, mostly men but a few women, shuffled out of the room, followed by the doctor.

The nurse asked me what I needed. A shower. That's what I needed. A shower and nothing else, no one else. I wanted to be alone.

I sat on the cement floor of the shower with the warm water pounding on my head. I had to get out of that hospital. I couldn't get clean. I thought of others who had suffered more, about books I'd read. Prisoners of war, the Jews in the Holocaust, what did they do? *Escape, you must escape. He was a doctor, right? It was a procedure, wasn't it? Why did I feel so filthy? Was it wrong? Why did it feel so wrong? I must escape.*

The medication made me throw up, an instant weight-loss program. When I alerted the doctors and the nurses, they didn't change the medication or dose. I hid the pills in my food or flushed them down the toilet. I'd already lost ten pounds in a few days. I feared they'd kill me. Meanwhile, a woman dying of cancer screamed in pain all night long in the room next door. I prayed for her.

Eileen, home from college on Christmas break, picked me up from the hospital. In my family, this happened often—as soon as the older ones could drive, Mom enlisted them to play chauffer for the younger ones.

I vomited in every trash can as we left the building. Eileen watched in disbelief.

"Julie, you're still sick. Maybe we should go back."

"No." I wiped the spittle from my mouth with the back of my hand. "I'm going home." She shook her head, drove, and urged me to roll down the window and hang my head out. Mom would kill me if I threw up all over the car.

For all my mom's classes in psychology, she didn't ask, and I didn't tell. How could she have suspected such a thing? I didn't tell anyone—not my mom, not Eileen, not even my best friend Karen—not a word. I didn't plot this out, this vow of silence. Something in my brain decided for me, sealed my shame in a vault. I felt violated, but at the same time not sure if the doctor did something wrong. The interns and nurses watched; no one objected. The procedure seemed standard; the doctor didn't perform the Pap smear in secret. Was the problem with me or the doctor?

If this happened at age twenty or thirty, I might've known to defend myself. *Pap smear? Are you kidding? Who gives a Pap smear for lung cancer?* The doctor never would've dared to ask. But he knew, at fifteen, he had me. The incident rocked my sense of order, the balance of right and wrong in my world, and my ability to tell the difference. So instead of questioning his actions, I ignored them as well as my feelings about what happened. If I didn't talk about the incident, didn't cry, maybe it didn't happen. Maybe then I might feel clean again, purged of his fingers, the metal, and his wet, thick voice in my ear. I ignored the doctor's actions and let one afternoon shape my life instead. I buried the hurt, buried it deep. My silence gave pain roots.

We moved about six months after my bout with pneumonia, but I went back periodically to Annandale. My friendship with Karen drifted. She became an evangelical involved with Young Life, while I changed my clothing from bright colors to black, smoked cigarettes, and began to sneak booze.

On one trip back, I stood in front of our old house and looked at the daffodils. Dad had planted them in the front yard, where they'd multiplied to produce a sea of yellow. I summoned the courage to knock on the door and ask to see the inside. The new owner welcomed me, thinking it odd that a high school senior would stop to reminisce.

"Do you mind if I look at my old room?"

"Sure." the woman opened the door. "Which one?"

"I'll show you." I bounded up the stairs, anticipating those amber tones, the tiny room, and the closet with the bare bulb. I made a quick right at the top of the stairs and turned into the open doorway. I caught my breath. The room wasn't yellow anymore. My stomach turned a notch beyond queasy. They had painted the room blue. I couldn't breathe. *It's just a room. Get a hold of yourself.* My body trembled.

"The morning sun just blasts through the window—unbearably hot. We painted it blue for a cooler effect. What do you think—" The woman must've noticed my eyes filling with tears.

My mouth opened but nothing came out—only wispy gasps. I ran down both sets of stairs and through the sliding glass doors to the backyard. I didn't stop until I reached my oak tree. Tears poured out, my shoulders shaking. Over my shoulder I could see the woman at the back door, calling after me. I hid, ashamed. The house was hers now. I couldn't paint the room yellow, move back in, and hide in the closet with my journal. I knew that, but I still hurt. I waited for the wind, the branches motionless. I wanted the light dance to lift my thoughts, to scatter my tears in the cloudless sky.

9

Patterns

I tied my running shoes and set out early, 5:00 a.m. The moon welcomed me, not the sun. I think my best thoughts in the morning, before the mad rush of breakfast on the go, the lost shoe, and the bad hair day that needs extra-strength mousse. Once the rest of the world wakes up, my day is shared with others, my concentration scattered in increments of minutes, sometimes less. On my run, my thoughts are mine alone. I focus and solve problems without the clamor of other voices.

I sprinted out the front gate. The story of the doctor jostled around in my brain. After the incident happened, I told no one for six years. My secret spilled out to my college roommate, by accident, after several beers.

"That's rape." Her prelaw eyes burned with anticipation. "We should get this guy." *Rape?* I argued with her—after all, didn't rape involve a penis? She assured me otherwise.

I breathed in. Cool air, perfect for running. I turned the corner, took in the dogwoods, blossoms broad and white in a fenced yard. In Virginia, dogwoods grow wild, the forest thick with them behind my Annandale house. Dallas doesn't have the right soil for dogwoods—too much clay and usually too much sun. This family found the right blend of dirt that I hadn't discovered.

The gravel crunched beneath my feet. I knew the doctor at Bethesda wasn't "it"—he wasn't the reason I ended up in a locked psychiatric ward. Sure, the experience hurt. Sure, I needed to heal those old wounds. But something more, something else, put me in Zale Lipshy. I lived a productive life for years after that day at Bethesda. I graduated from college, held a job, made friends, had a life, and succeeded by anyone's terms.

One incident at age fifteen didn't plunge me into clinical depression.

Headlights glared behind me. I jumped to the side of the road to let the car pass.

In the months after ECT, I began to pick apart my life like a scientist. *Where is the data? What are the trends? Has this happened before?* Yes. Depression hit my freshman year at Notre Dame, after the breakup with the hockey player, when I got shin splints from the ice and couldn't run. I shivered. My freshman year at Notre Dame was exceptionally brutal, too rough for a Virginia girl who needed the right soil like her dogwoods.

Gray from November to May.

Could the weather really make a difference? Part of me scoffed at this. Ridiculous! I'd read about Seasonal Affective Disorder, SAD. I began to wonder—did gray weather become the catalyst for my depression? I gathered the data. Two major depressions—did cloudy skies accompany both? Yes. Both initiated in January, one in the gray Midwest, the other in an unseasonably rainy Dallas. Maybe sunlight, or lack thereof, caused some sort of chemical reaction. Still, SAD seemed an incomplete answer.

I suppressed anger and hurt, and I knew that led to depression. *What do I do instead of working things out? Why?*

I turned another corner, and a white dog snarled at the edge of his invisible fence, barked his warning. I ran a little faster.

That's it. That's what I do. I speed up to forget things. I sped up to deal with my grief about Karen, which led to pneumonia. After the doctor incident, I sped up again. Did I speed up at Notre Dame?

I turned the corner for the last half mile, a straight stretch. *So that's it? Bad weather. Crisis. Speed up. Don't get help?* I'd need to test my hypothesis, to think about the first time I experienced depression. I entered the house and beelined to my office, curious to see what I wrote in my journal for the winter after Becka was born, the second highest rainfall on record in Dallas. I didn't remember being depressed, only busy. With an infant and an active two-year-old, I was exhausted. I paged through the journals. Nothing for almost three years. Not surprising. With two children under the age of four, I never wrote. Solitude didn't exist.

I closed the journal. *I need to find the patterns. I need to go back to the first time my depression surfaced.* The first time. Notre Dame, winter of my freshman year. For me, a person who thought of winter as December through February with a few snow days in between, the chill I experienced at Notre Dame was colder, grayer, and deeper than I ever expected.

10

Winter in South Bend

*J*ules, I don't feel the same anymore." He looked away, green eyes dull, none of the spark that lured me in September. "I'm having an affair with a thirty-year-old divorced woman."

"What?" I backed up, bumped into my dorm bed. I lowered myself; I sat while he stood. Was he kidding? Where does a nineteen-year-old college freshman meet divorcees?

He leaned against the porcelain sink, his back to the mirror, and crossed his arms. "She hung out after my games, followed the team on the road." His voice sounded a world away, as though he called the words to me from the end of a long, dark tunnel. "Jules, are you okay?"

I caught my reflection in the mirror. Eighteen years old. Pale. Dark brows, dark hair to my shoulders. He gave me a pink cashmere sweater for Christmas. I never wore pink, but I wore that sweater. The color made my skin glow. *I bet she's beautiful. Good in bed.*

"Jules?" He'd been my protector since the fall, strong, agile, light on his feet. He gave me confidence. "Jules, I'm sorry, but this is how it has to be." He leaned forward, held my arms, and kissed me on the forehead like a child. He looked worried. "Are you okay? Can I call someone?" I shook my head no. He turned toward the door and looked back over his shoulder. "I'm sorry."

"It's okay," I lied. "I'll be fine."

The breakup was the catalyst to my first depressive breakdown. Stresses, like timber, collected one by one. I'd made Dean's List first semester, but by December I knew I could never survive a pre-med curriculum. The intense focus that carried me the first semester wavered. I didn't know who I wanted to be. My grades slipped. Gray weather. I got shin splints from running on the ice and hung up my shoes for the winter. More gray weather. Grades slipped further. The breakup struck like a match.

In the fall, running had been my antidote, a sedative for my nervous stomach. I ran to settle myself. One side of my head scrambled, trying to find a time slot for every piece of work. The other side whispered as each foot hit the ground, *You can do it. You can do it. Just keep at it.* As the temperature dropped, mist rose from the lakes and mingled with the bright yellow leaves.

The following January in South Bend, the snow piled on the side of the road, heavy on the trees, on the side of the sidewalks as I trudged to class. The plowed snow had lines, gray and black, that showed the number of previous snowfalls, like aged layers of sandstone. Gray, bitter, endless winter. I'd never experienced cold like that. The inside of my nose iced over with a step outside. When I touched metal with naked fingertips, I left prints of skin as evidence of my southern naiveté.

I stopped eating. I stopped sleeping. I skipped classes, disillusioned at first and then terminally behind. *Why work so hard? For what?* I didn't know what I wanted to be, so why try? Without extra effort, I couldn't keep up. My strength in academia never relied on my quickness but my endurance. Finally, as I tend to do when stressed beyond my breaking point, I sped up.

Without the benefit of food, exercise, or sleep, I began to see things and connect coincidences. The gothic structure of the buildings at Notre Dame took on a sinister air, and I began to imagine voices in dark corners. Sometimes I saw things, beings or ghostlike creatures. I'd shake my head, and they'd disappear. I didn't tell anyone about this until much later, when the illusions overtook me. I knew whoever I told would think I was crazy.

As I slipped further, I made fast friendships with strangers, some very strange. One, a six feet six inch tall student magician, asked me to be his assistant. My roommate advised me to avoid him. Get some sleep, eat some food, and hit the books. I ignored her. Within a few days, the illusion escalated. The magician was possessed; he wanted to possess me. I saw satanic symbols on his door.

I ran from him, took the stairs by twos. I stood in the middle of the North Quad, in front of my dorm. "Someone help me. Please. Help me!" I watched the plumes of smoke rise from my mouth in the January air. I pleaded with God. "What do you want from me? Why don't you help?" The wind blew and rattled the leafless trees, but I heard no answer. I fell on the hard concrete, knees first, and held my head in my hands.

No one helped. I screamed, and no one rushed to my side. Or at least I thought I screamed. At Notre Dame, with a three-to-one male-female ratio, there were plenty of desperate men on the lookout for damsels in distress. Especially a datable damsel. My guess is if I'd screamed out loud, I would've caused a stampede. The screams were silent, inside my head. At age eighteen, induced by lack of sleep and food, I had my first psychotic episode.

The next morning, my hands shaking, I picked up the phone and called my mother.

"Hello?" My voice caught.

"Hello? Are you there?"

"Mom, it's me. I need to come home."

"What? Wait a minute, let me turn down Donohue." Mom religiously watched Phil Donohue when she folded laundry.

"Julie, what's the problem? You are coming home, remember? Spring break."

"Now. Mom, I need to come home now."

"What? Today? Are you hurt?"

"No."

"Is this about that hockey player? That jerk. Why'd he break up with you anyway?" She paused. "You didn't sleep with him, did you?"

"Mom, I need to come home, please."

"Come on, Julie, whatever it is, hang in there. We—"

"Mom, I can't—"

"Can't afford it, you know that. We don't—"

"I can't make it," I whispered. The tears rolled from my eyes and dripped onto the receiver.

"We can't spend money like that. You have to keep moving. If you leave midsemester, you won't be able to finish the year. You've got to stick it out."

Stick it out. The Family Credo. As predictable as *Don't be a quitter* and *Take your vitamins.*

Mom seemed distracted. She told me Grandma was staying at our house. Grandma's strokes had left her hand curled in an arch, words out of reach. I didn't tell Mom about the magician or the satanic symbols on the door. I wasn't sure what was real and what wasn't. Besides, Mom had her hands full.

"Promise me you'll try, even for a few days."

I knew that tone. It didn't matter what I promised.

"Come on, you'll be okay." A doorbell rang in the background. "Damn, someone's at the front door. Promise me?"

"Mom—"

"I know you'll be okay." She yelled "just a minute" to the person at the door. "I'll call you later, Julie. I love you."

The phone clicked on the other end.

My hands cradled the phone and waited for some hint about what to do next. A voice sprinkled its advice through the receiver—"Your call cannot be connected as dialed. Please hang up and try again." I hung up the phone, went to my desk drawer, rummaged for a pen, and pulled down my journal from the bookshelf. The last entry's date was over two months ago. My words lathered about the hockey player and that damn pink sweater he gave me for Christmas.

My pen dug into the paper as I crafted my list.

1. Eat.

2. Get seven hours of sleep a night.

3. Run fifteen miles a week.

4. Pray at least twenty minutes a day.

My journals are filled with lists. The list changes, but for most of my young life "lose ten pounds" got top billing. I'd made the list often enough at New Year's, on birthdays, in times of crisis. The process became its own ritual.

I wrote as if the speed might promote my recovery. Though the ritual seemed familiar, something felt different, more desperate. I was shaken; I no longer trusted my gut. This was no momentary panic, no challenge to hone my skills for a great adventure. I was lost. Worse still, the traits I assumed were my strengths—a level head, determination, and savvy—dissolved before my eyes. I gnawed the top of my pen as I read and reread my four-point checklist.

I'd never commanded myself to eat, and the word looked foreign at the top of my list. Those extra ten pounds had disappeared and left me without my natural insulation. As the scale edged close to a hundred pounds, my body weight slipped to as low as when I'd left the hospital with pneumonia, over three years before. Many people could be five feet one inch at that weight and look fine, but I felt lean, brittle, without reserve. My skin flaked and had a strange gray color no matter how much lotion I applied. I was sucked dry. Even so, I wrote my list of improvements and repeated it to myself like some four-step, self-help mantra.

In the next four weeks, I avoided the oversized magician and ate large clumps of peanut butter directly off a spoon. I needed to gain weight. The thick smell followed me, left its scent on my guitar long after I washed my hands. My guitar became my voice through February and into March; the minor chords sounded fears I couldn't quantify. Gloomy verses emerged as I strummed. *They bound my mother's words with chains. They kicked my father 'til now he is lame.* I wrote the lyrics of a '60s revolutionary lost in the wrong decade. My anger bludgeoned every form of authority—the Catholic Church, Notre Dame, the government—but not me. I never labeled what happened as psychotic or wondered if counseling or medication might help. I was eighteen and clearly oppressed. Genes, stress, and bad weather didn't make good lyrics.

I lived on edge. My body burned food at an unprecedented rate, as though catapulted into some unknown high gear. I attended class and went to the library. *Look normal,* I told myself, whatever that is. I can't imagine I fooled anyone, but no one challenged me. No one ever suggested I see a counselor, even after I spilled the possession story to my rectress. Instead, she prayed with me, a *Hail Mary*.

I didn't know what plagued me, but I refused to investigate. I moved on, worked harder. *Ignore it. Deny it. Bury it.* I didn't know who I was or what I should be, and the unanswered questions made me nuts.

At the same time, the rest of the world held an invisible stopwatch that required my immediate decision. *Pick a major. Go to class. Graduate and get a job. Don't stop or you can't keep up.*

When I went home for spring break, I pleaded for a year off. I never saw a counselor or a doctor. My parents considered college major angst and romantic breakups minor stepping-stones to adulthood, problems everyone faced, unworthy of a counselor's fee. Completing the year, however wobbly, stood paramount.

I returned to school after spring break to finish the year in a frantic effort to catch up. Chemistry, taught by Professor Emil T. Hofman, left me dumbfounded. I knocked on Hofman's door and begged him to let me skip the final exam. He laughed and asked me to think about my career. I told him I wanted to be a writer. Hofman's jowls eased into an uncharacteristic upward arch. He looked sad but knowing, as if he'd had the same conversation with someone else. "You've got to live first, so you have something to write about."

Between my breakup and my GPA crash, I learned there was a whole universe of things I couldn't do. By the last exam, the high-wire energy that kept me suspended for months snapped. When I drove home from school with a friend that year, I struggled to stay awake. White lines flashed on the black road in the dark. They matched the beat in my head. *Failed. Failed. What now?*

That summer, I visited my family doctor because I hadn't had a period in over four months.

"Could you be pregnant?" Dr. Blackburn asked.

"Look, I haven't had sex in six months. Unless this is the second coming, I'm not pregnant."

Blackburn laughed. "Have you ever heard of depression?"

I was over the hockey player. I got through school. I passed chemistry, with a D, but who was counting. "Depression? What's that got to do with my period?"

"You're abnormally thin. That'd do it, but that's not what worries me."

"What?"

"You've stressed your body to an unhealthy state. Your liver function looks bad; you look worn out. You're only nineteen; you can't keep this up. Drink less . . . let your mother take care of you."

"Great."

"Don't try to do everything yourself."

Do what all by myself? Mom wasn't going to wait on me. Dad couldn't take my exams. *What did he mean by that?* He patted me on the shoulder and left the room for his next appointment.

He didn't hand me a card for a counselor. In 1979, in a small town, it wasn't done. These days, a local doc might whip out a prescription for Zoloft or Paxil and treat depression like an allergy or a toe fungus. I'm not sure that's a better solution. A broken spirit doesn't magically heal with pills or home cooking. So I listened to my doctor and tried to eat myself to health. I ate and ate and ate, as if mounds of food might smother the depression out of my body.

Having gone from about 100 pounds to 110 over the summer, I began my sophomore year. I switched majors to business, not my choice, but again Dad set the tone. Not wanting to support his five children financially after they left school, Dad demanded practical majors. English or other liberal arts endeavors were viewed as the candy of an undergraduate experience, not the main course. We settled on a major in marketing, focusing all my electives in English. During my sophomore year in business, however, no electives appeared on the schedule. I looked at my fall semester of classes with dread—accounting, statistics, finance, and economics. I ate some more. I dated a guy who called me Pork Chop.

It was a long year. I stared at my books, bored, unable to absorb anything. A midafternoon Snickers bar and a Tab revved my brain for about a half-hour, and then I returned to the same dull state, aimlessly flipping pages. I ran. I drank. My boyfriend screwed his Pork Chop in the back of a station wagon after pitchers of beer. No matter what happened, I felt wrapped in a thick layer of gauze. My grades plunged from Dean's List to the low two-point range for three semesters. By the end of my sophomore year, I had gained close to fifty pounds.

That summer, something stopped the perpetual slide. Maybe the blue Virginia sky helped. The depression lifted slowly, invisibly. According to one psychiatrist, I'm not alone in this; most cases of clinical depression resolve themselves in less than a year, with or without medication. Time is the key. The trick is whether or not the depressed person can wait out the bleak period or find an antidepressant that works before thoughts become deadly. Luckily, for me the depression lifted without medicine or therapy.

I started to run again, up a hill by my house. The dirt road I took wove a mile straight up, past a turkey farm. The first few times I ran the hill, I stopped multiple times, bent over at the waist, sucking air. By the end of the summer, I could take the hill without strain. The pounds dropped off. I worked at a dinner theater and pulled in great tips. A boy wrote me a poem and gave me a bouquet of four-leaf clovers. My luck seemed to change, and I changed with it.

With new interest, I chose electives for my junior year—British Writers, Modern Poets, Mysticism, and Poetry Writing. More pounds dropped. I reached 115, my ideal weight. I'd maintain this weight, give or take five pounds, for the next fourteen years, until I had my first child. My body felt right and my brain followed. Balanced with courses that ignited a fire in my brain, my core business courses no longer worked as a sedative. Somehow, quantitative methods seemed easy, though statistics baffled me the year before. The transition defied logic. I dumped my boyfriend; I no longer saw myself as Pork Chop material. Completing the pendulum swing, I made the Dean's List. I stabilized to a steady pace.

South Bend's winter seemed less brutal that year, and by the time spring came, I felt strong again. Fed with Keats, Frost, Shakespeare, and Tennyson, I no longer ate my peanut butter by the spoonful. I found my soul food. I feasted on plays, poetry, and stories. In the spring of that year, I didn't focus on gray skies and frozen ground—instead, I noticed daffodils that peeked through the snow. The landscape of South Bend remained the same, but I looked with new eyes.

II

Dad

*T*ell me about your father." Dr. Yvonne leaned back in her chair. "Do you ever dream about him?" A Jungian analyst, Dr. Yvonne used dreams to understand her patients.

I pulled a loose thread on my sweater. "Not much anymore." For a long time after his death, I had nightmares. Finally I dreamed that I tilted his hospital bed so he could see the sunrise. After that, Dad appeared in a more familiar form. Lean. Strong. Determined.

"Anything recent?"

The thread went taut in the middle of the sweater. I let go. "The last one I remember, he apologized." I felt tears in my eyes. *Damn it! I want to get through one session without crying.*

Dr. Yvonne shifted toward the box of tissues on her table. "For what?"

"He told me he did me a disservice." My dad and I never reached a comfortable age together. About the time I could accept him and he could accept me, he died. Dad never met my husband, never met my son whose muscular build matches his.

"Disservice?"

"He told me I was supposed to write."

We loved each other, but we also frustrated each other. Athletic, hardworking, and organized, Dad's priorities stood clear. I felt Dad's disapproval of my body and my interests. If I misread him, he told me. My Little Butterball. Get some exercise. Poet's starve. Why don't you go into sales? You'd be a great salesperson.

Early in my dating years, Dad maintained a quiet distance. When I reached my twenties, however, he monitored my love life with close interest. Dad's parental advice cranked to high volume.

Close to graduation at Notre Dame, Augrhim Furey begged me to join him on a yearlong round-the-world trip. At twenty-one, marriage seemed a speck on a distant horizon. *Will Auggie marry me? Who cares? I love the guy.*

Dad pummeled me with the minuses of my carefree approach. You'll never be able to secure a job. You might get pregnant. Do you think he'll marry you? Why buy the cow when the milk is free? I winced at the cliché, sure that Dad didn't understand the depth of my relationship. Auggie loved me. We loved the same things—the outdoors, literature, and art. I felt this guy was my soul mate.

Dad remained unconvinced. Ultimately, he influenced my decision. I took a high-tech job with Osborne Computer Corporation, the manufacturer of the first portable computer, which weighed in at twenty-six pounds. Auggie left to circle the globe. Abstinence imposed by absence failed to make our hearts grow fonder. The relationship dissolved within a few months.

My volatile work life didn't bother Dad, even though I worked with three different companies in less than three years. Silicon Valley, in the early '80s, was the wild west of the business world. My father enjoyed my work stories; he always championed capitalism in motion. Dad possessed an entrepreneurial spirit. Risk didn't scare him. Risk for his children didn't upset him. Risk with low upside, however, collided with his logic.

A career in the arts or writing fell into the high-risk/low-reward category. Dad directed me toward what he considered reasonable life choices. Write as a hobby. Marry someone you love, but who also has a steady job. Coming from poverty, Dad feared my attraction to men and interests that forecasted little chance of ever generating cash.

As a business analyst in high tech, I helped salespeople clinch deals worth thousands, sometimes millions, of dollars. I sat in my office after one of these sales calls. With my ace product knowledge, I wowed another customer to the wonders of voicemail and nonsimultaneous communication. Rocking side to side in my chair, I replayed the meeting in my head. Damn, I was good.

I turned on my computer and launched the word processor to write my report for my boss. My fingers rattled on the keyboard, certain I could solve anything. When the phone rang, I plucked the receiver from its cradle and crooked it on my shoulder.

"This is Julie, how can I help you?"

"Hey, Jules. It's Patrick." I straightened. My brother never called me at the office.

"It's about Dad."

"Did they find something? How bad?" I felt the energy draining from my core, as though the news sucked my life force into the phone.

"Bad. Mom's really upset. She'd call you herself but—"

"What the hell is it?" The phone sat silent. "Tell me. Now."

Patrick cleared his throat. "He's got cancer. They're not sure where it started."

I felt dizzy, reached for my can of Diet Coke. Empty. "He's not going to die, is he?" Tears filled my eyes. I brushed them back. Damn you, Dad, you can't die on me. I'm not done with you yet. "Can't they do something?"

"They're trying chemotherapy. There's a chance."

I took a breath, realized I hadn't been breathing. "A chance, that's good, right? So there's some hope . . ."

"Some," Patrick said, "but he might die in eight months. We need to prepare—"

"Dad will fight. He'll live."

I couldn't hear Patrick on the other end of the phone.

"Patrick?"

"I hope so."

"I know so. Dad will survive. He's more stubborn than anyone. The jerk never let me win a tennis match."

At age twenty-four, I learned my father would be dead in eight months. The X-rays showed masses in his stomach and throughout his abdominal area. Some people survived cancer as advanced as his, but not many. The doctor gave him his prescription—get your life in order, say your good-byes, and pray. He was fifty-eight years old.

My current boyfriend and I flew to Kitty Hawk, North Carolina, the first time in years that my family gathered in the same place at the same time. No longer kids, my siblings' ages ranged from twenty-two to thirty-four. My three older siblings were married; my sister Eileen brought her son, the only grandchild at the time. We caught flights from San Francisco, San Diego, and Atlanta and then drove the narrow roads from Norfolk for a show of family force. My family might forget birthdays or not call for months, but if there's a crisis, we're a reliable crew. Battle trained. Battle ready. The Captain's children. Bring it on.

That summer was the last time I'd see my father in a comparable version of his former self. Dad looked worn, thinner than usual, but remained functional. He walked to the beach and ate dinner with us. He even swam in the ocean.

One night he pulled out a workbook he'd gathered at a life-planning seminar. He handed a copy to each of us, with a No. 2 pencil, sharpened, and called a family meeting. The packet asked questions about life goals, priorities, ambitions, and percentages of time. He asked us to fill out the form.

"Now?" I set down my form. *We've traveled from all parts of the country to take a test?* "How about a conversation?" I felt the buzz of several glasses of wine. Patrick, Eileen, and Matt leafed through the workbook, with their spouses looking over their shoulders. Teddy, still single, paged through his by himself.

"I'll do this later." I grabbed my boyfriend's hand and led him to the deck at the top of the house. We looked at the stars and said nothing. The silence between us wasn't profound or deep or even abnormal; silence formed the bulk of our conversations. My boyfriend had smoked a joint before dinner. He always had his joint in the evenings, like a cocktail. By 8:00 p.m., he never said much.

The next day at the beach we applied sunscreen, read our books, and bobbed in the waves. The waves carried us far up onto the beach, not too rough, but strong enough for a good ride. Dad loved the water. He dove under frothy crests and emerged unscathed. He pinched and played the shark. The two of us caught a wave. We were knocked hard. I staggered to my feet and laughed, my suit full of sand.

Dad hobbled on his hands and knees a few yards away from me, closer to where the waves broke. Another wave leveled him. The situation didn't register at first. Dad didn't have the strength to pull himself up. I ran to where he struggled, again too close to the break point. I grabbed his arm. The waves hit my back and pulled us both down. I wouldn't let go. I struggled to my feet and pulled him up with me. In my hands, his arm seemed so frail, all bone and withered muscle. His right arm hung limp, the arm that once spun cheap shots and nailed the back line of the court. He coughed, sputtered, and smiled. "I guess I've got to be more careful."

The future still uncertain, my grip tightened. I dragged my father to a spot where I felt safe, high on the beach, where the dry sand stuck to his skin. Sometimes I wonder if I did the right thing that day. He could've died more quickly, with less pain.

When I caught the plane back to San Francisco, I noticed Dad's life analysis form in the carrying case I brought on the plane. I never filled in the blanks. Dad planned his life, carefully. He sacrificed for his family. He saved his money to help put his children through college. Now, with the military pension and a university salary, he'd hit the financial jackpot. But what did money matter? He was dying.

Dying at fifty-eight. Shouldn't those numbers be reversed? Shouldn't fathers live to eighty-five and see their children married with children? I left the life analysis form in the pocket of the seat in front of me. Screw planning. Life happens. Death happens. Not when you plan Death, but when Death feels like it, whether you're ready or not.

At Christmas, four months later, I returned to my parents' home in Harrisonburg, not knowing what to expect, but not expecting what I saw. Mom said things were worse. A measurement in November proved the tumors grew despite the brutal doses of chemotherapy.

Still, I tried to think positively. He might get better. Dad was Dad, after all. Dad could do anything.

A fire crackled in the living room when I arrived. Dad lay on the couch in a plaid flannel shirt covered with blankets. He'd lost all his thick, dark hair except for a few straggling wisps at the top of his head. His face had shrunk to cheekbones, his wide eyes, and the broad expanse of his Polish nose. When I entered, his hazel eyes brightened and his smile grew wide, overtaking his face. He held out his arms and struggled to stand. I knew then he was going to die. Soon.

We had a good Christmas that year, the first one we'd all spent together in more than ten years. We toasted, ate, and broke oplatek on Christmas Eve. Sharing oplatek is a Polish custom. The father takes a piece of unleavened wafer, similar to an unconsecrated host, breaks a piece with each member of the family, and makes each one a wish for the New Year. The family members then take their pieces and break them for each other, also making wishes. The custom offers a time of forgiveness, reconciliation. One by one, we hugged Dad good-bye, wondering if we'd see him alive again.

We all had jobs, bills—our own lives that demanded our attention. The Family and Medical Leave Act didn't exist yet. I'd already taken time off at Christmas. I worried if I stayed in Harrisonburg through January I'd lose my job. With no savings, I couldn't pay rent without work. High tech stops for no one—capitalism at its best. I flew back to California and drove to San Jose on Monday morning.

Back at work, I listened to a customer scream about the flaws in his call accounting system. I felt myself float off and the voice blur. You missed a call and can't bill back, that's, well, serious stuff. Yes, I realize your company can't make money if you can't bill. I understand you're upset. Right, right, you want it fixed. Now.

I want my problem fixed too. I just realized I'll never see my father plant another bulb. He was so careful with those bulbs, first the deep hole, then the bone meal before he placed the bulb in its tomb and gently pushed the dirt on top. He grew tomatoes, azaleas, tulips, but I loved the daffodils the best. Bright, big trumpets, blasting yellow with no apology. Daffodils did nothing quantifiable, tangible. Dad fostered something that had no real purpose except to be, to bring color to an otherwise monotonous landscape. Flowers were my father's art. When I saw those bright colors, our connection made sense. I understood I came from him.

Dad almost lived through January but not quite. I left work and spent close to a month with him. My brothers Patrick and Teddy joined me for the final weeks. We took shifts sitting with Dad in the hospice, waiting for each day to be his last.

Dad sensed our tension and played tricks on us to help us regain our sense of humor. One day when Patrick and I sat on either side of him, Dad raised his head weakly.

"Well, now, I guess I can't delay anymore. I guess this is it."

Patrick and I panicked, tried to think of the perfect last words for a man dying. Dad absorbed our anxiety and smiled.

"I guess I need to take my medicine." Dad reminded us daily, in his own way, that he wasn't in the ground yet.

Teddy, Patrick, and I worked on a poem for Dad's funeral. I'd started the poem and asked for their help.

Looking back, I see my Dad
Placing bulbs in tombs of clay.

Patrick looked at the first line. *"We, not I. We see our Dad,* from all of us."

I changed the words and wrote the best I could. More than a single word change is needed to represent five views of the same person. Each of us saw him differently, some of my siblings closer than others, but me, at least from my perspective, the most distant. We all loved him and felt cheated, our time cut short.

The night before he died, I sat with Dad all night. I felt death in the room and didn't want him to die alone. Morning came. I fought to keep my eyes open. As Dad lay on the bed, comatose, mouth held open like a little bird, I read him the poem my brothers and I wrote. I told him I'd read the poem at his funeral. I thanked him for a great life. I told him I knew he'd die before I got back, and that was okay. "Love you, Dad."

His breathing continued, labored, with no answer, but I knew. I walked to the door and listened to his breath until I reached the hall. I had to eat something, sleep, move.

He died about four hours later. In the middle of my haircut, the phone rang and the stylist went white, looked down at her shoes. She handed me the phone, and Mom explained he died about fifteen minutes earlier. I glanced at my watch but couldn't read the numbers.

The call ended, and the stylist asked if she should stop cutting. My ends were mismatched: a good two-inch difference in length. I told her to finish. I watched my dark hair scatter on the pattern of the linoleum, trying not to feel relief. I couldn't have lasted another day watching Dad battle for such a pitiful existence. At the same time, I already missed him.

When I got back to the hospice, Mom, Teddy, and Patrick talked about Dad's last few minutes as the nurse pulled the sheets from his bed. She came to turn Dad, and he died in her arms. No sudden burst of consciousness, no last words, just a strained breath followed by the absence of breathing.

He died without me. I told him he could. All those hours I gently cradled his hand and Dad chose to die when a nurse pushed him over. His last breath, shared with her, seemed a strange sort of infidelity.

At the wake, people filled the chapel, stood in the back. People told stories about how Dad helped them, believed in them, and inspired them. One man told the story about his summer camp for underprivileged children. Dad had helped him, coached him on how to finance the summer camp. "No one listened but Professor . . ." His voice broke.

Dad helped the man get financing, and his camp thrived. "He was the only one who believed in me," the man sobbed, a grown man, tears in an avalanche. I'd never met him. *How could someone love my father so much and I don't know his name?* Joe, Dad, Naval Captain, University Professor—my dad lived several lives simultaneously.

My brother Matt talked about how Dad always tossed the baseball with him even though Dad knew he'd never be a professional baseball player. Eileen recalled how Dad could fix anything. He only needed a book and the right tools. Mom told the story about seeing Dad for the first time, in his baggy pants. I talked about his sense of humor, how he teased us until the very end, pretending to die when it was time to take his medicine.

I hurt, and as I do when I hurt, I sped up. Frenzied, I planned the funeral, picked the songs, made the final edits to our poem, and designed the service. While I read the poem, each of my siblings brought a token to the altar that represented something Dad loved: Teddy the spade for gardening, Patrick a graduation cap for education, Matt his flight jacket for his pilot years, Eileen a shell for the beach, and Mom a daffodil.

Mom complained about the daffodil and wanted a more important role. Mom didn't see that the daffodil meant rebirth, resurrection, that the "smallest sprout shows there is really no death. And if ever there was it led forward to life." Mom never cared for Walt Whitman. I tried to explain the flower's meaning to her with no success but forced her to carry the daffodil anyway.

I wanted to read that poem without tears, loud enough for everyone to hear. When I reached the part about Dad jumping in the waves with us, I glanced at my brother Matt. Holding his chin up, he motioned me to continue. I thought of the beach, sun, laughter, the smell of salt and coconut lotion. Dad as the shark, the sand stuck to his back. "I've got to be more careful." Eileen put the seashell on the altar, and my voice broke. I tasted salt on my lips. Dad taught me to dive under waves and burst through safely on the other side. A seashell on an altar didn't do his lessons justice.

They buried him in Arlington Cemetery. His last wish. Full military funeral, black horses with the casket draped in a flag, gunshots over his grave. A simple white headstone, among so many other white headstones.

Matt, then a young Navy lieutenant, saluted the casket while the snow danced against his dark uniform. The snow fell lightly on my face, stinging cold. After the soldiers folded the flag with razor-sharp intensity, they handed it to my mother. She thanked them, even though a flag is a poor trade for a dead husband.

Dad's body now lies in a field with thousands of other men and women whose end of life surprised them. Although Dad didn't take a bullet for his country, his death felt the same. Cancer meanders more than a bullet, taking time. A bullet stuns. Cancer pulls bystanders by both arms until they snap. Both ends left me looking at graves in disbelief. The starting and ending dates, carved in stone, seemed too close together.

Dad preached about freedom and justice, but he never mentioned that sometimes the scales tip with a logic that escapes us. Sometimes the only comfort is the symmetry of a thousand stones on a lush, grassy hillside, each one chiseled with a name.

12

Pain Management

*T*he smell of garlic filled the Foster City apartment I shared with my fiancé. I closed the door behind me. Bob James and David Sanborn's "More than Friends" blasted so loud no one heard me enter. In the kitchen, two friends leaned against the counter. One rolled a joint.

"Hello, dear." Our friend Jimmy opened the refrigerator with a flourish. "Rough day at work? Would you like an ice-cold beverage?" Before I could answer, he popped the cap on a Miller Lite and placed the bottle in my hand.

I took a sip. "Where's Scooby?" We called my fiancé Scooby because he did a great imitation of the cartoon dog. Plus, the name fit.

Jimmy tilted his head toward the couch where Scooby inhaled a large slice of garlic pizza. His foot rested on the coffee table, next to a Frisbee.

I stepped toward Scooby, away from the kitchen. "Any luck with the job search today?" Snickers erupted behind my back.

"Rut Ro." Scooby made his red eyes round with mock surprise. "No one called me. Besides, we had a Frisbee tournament."

I slammed the beer down on the coffee table. "Have you picked your groomsmen?"

"Pick me! Pick me!" Jimmy fluttered in the room, put his fist on his hip and index finger to his lips, and then pointed. "Navy is my best color, but chartreuse might work."

A copy of *What Color Is Your Parachute?* sat unopened on top of the TV. Scooby had lost his job two months prior. We planned to marry in six months.

"Nice." I glared at Scooby. "Nice joke."

"Not everyone's like you—we can't all be workaholics."

"No chance of that." I marched to our bedroom, slammed the door behind me. No chance at all.

After my dad died, I decided I needed to grow up and get married. I never considered grief counseling. Instead, I filled my life with work and pressured my boyfriend to propose. Shortly after we were engaged, he lost his job. His unemployment didn't deter me, nor did his generous consumption of Miller Lite and pot. I figured I could change him. With that lifetime fixer-upper project, I'd never have time to slow down.

The engagement dissolved about four months before the wedding. Scooby's unemployment and the discovery of his lover in another city tipped me off that a life without marriage might be better than a marriage disaster. I broke the engagement. My friends and family breathed out, well aware my life had escaped a tragic detour. Eventually, I agreed. Still, I wanted a husband and felt I lagged behind schedule. All my older siblings married at twenty-six. At that age and without a prospect in sight, I saw my chance for my own family endangered.

I initiated relationships, each with a pathetic end. My friends teased me about having a reverse Midas touch. Several times I picked a man with a job or great potential. Within weeks of our initial date, my marriage candidate lost his job. Loyal to a fault, I supported my marriage candidates, sure each of them would eventually propose. None of them did.

On a whim, I called Auggie, my college soul mate from Notre Dame. The next week, I flew to Hawaii where he clerked as an intern. After a few days, he proposed on the beach at sunset. I said yes but then faltered. We'd been apart for six years. I wanted to make sure I still knew him.

With visions of love letters in my head, I suggested we take a month to get reacquainted. Auggie reluctantly agreed. I felt confident our love could span geographic distance. His letters, sporadic, bemoaned my lack of spontaneity. Auggie rescinded his offer in a few weeks. He told me he had "lost the feeling."

I spent more time at work. First in, last out, I clocked more hours than anyone, which takes special effort in the high-tech world. One night at about 8:00, my boss, Rick, approached my desk. Briefcase in hand, he was headed home.

Deep into a sort of the customer database I'd developed, I felt his lanky build lean against my cubicle.

"What are you still doing here?"

I didn't look up. "I'm almost done. Davis has some presentation tomorrow and he needs stats from our customer base."

Rick ground his teeth. "You've got to say no to them." Rick reported to Mike Davis. Davis went directly to me. All the executive staff occasionally contacted me with emergency tasks. I'd been with the company since the early days of its existence. With me, they could speak in shorthand. They knew if something needed to be done, I could execute it.

"No?" I squinted at him, eyes blurred from too many hours focused on the computer screen. "Are you kidding? I'm the only one who knows how to do this."

Rick shook his head and set down his briefcase. He grabbed a sticky note off my desk and wrote down a name and number. He handed the note to me. "Promise me you'll call this woman."

I glanced at the note, impatient. "What's she need?"

"Nothing. The number's for you. She's a counselor."

I snorted. My head hit the back of my chair. "What, you think I have issues?"

"No, you're going through a rough spot. You're here all the time. You're in your twenties." He bent down, retrieved his briefcase. "Do you ever have fun?"

"Let me get this straight." I laughed. "My boss is telling me I spend too much time at work?"

"I've seen her. She can help you."

I held the note up to my eyes. "Really?"

"Just try one session." He picked up his briefcase. "You can pay in cash. No one needs to know."

I went to two sessions. In the first, I cried for the entire hour. In the second, I babbled nonstop, excited about a date for the following weekend. I never went back. Medication? Never an option. I considered myself cured.

I entered the limbo world of late twenty-something life, a single career woman sobered by too many relationships gone south. I made my list in my journal—lose ten pounds, stop drinking, meditate, learn to like being alone.

At work, I'd spout my new single person's mission, confident in my choice. At night, alone in my little condo, I cried. One night the tears wouldn't stop. My life seemed so bitter, so lonely, framed by the idea I'd never have children, never grow old with someone who shared my life. I fell into sleep and my tears continued.

I stood in my dream, sobbing. I felt warmth, a presence from behind me. A man embraced me. He stood at my back and his hands crossed at my waist. Without words, he reassured me that I would be healed. Healed. The word seemed foreign, not mine. He put the thought in my head without speaking. A bright light surrounded his arms and fingertips as he hugged me. I never saw his face, or heard a voice, but I could tell the being was male—and short—because my head hit his shoulder when I leaned against him.

Who was this man? My father? Some Christ figure? My sense was that whoever he was, I didn't know him yet, but he was waiting for me. When he touched me, I felt a sense of wholeness, contentment. With his touch, my problems dissipated. I woke optimistic, wondering who he was.

I met Ken at a Stanford MBA Halloween party, a party neither of us planned to attend. When a Stanford intern in our marketing group invited my friend Kristi and me to the party, I told him no thanks. I'd interviewed several Stanford interns for jobs at Octel, the high-tech company where I worked. Stanford MBAs were too arrogant, too uptight, and too young for my taste.

Kristi pleaded with me, suggesting that we wear hideous costumes to avoid contact from unwanted males. She wanted a night out. Kristi went as Dana Carvey's "Church Lady" character from *Saturday Night*

Live, complete with narrow glasses, an overpadded butt, a button-down sweater, and a walk that matched the outfit. I pulled my hair back, donned a large brimmed, pointed straw hat, baggy black clothes, and claimed myself a Chinese peasant farmer.

Ken arrived to the party dressed as a cowboy. We exchanged the standard introductory questions—what's your name, where are you from, do you dance—but not much more. He had planned to leave early, but he lost the directions to the other party he wanted to attend. Ken rarely loses anything—this night proved an exception for both of us.

Ken called me after the party for a date. At first I didn't remember who he was, but his candor and cleverness over the phone impressed me. I turned him down, already booked with another person. He persisted and called again. He charmed me. I said yes.

When I opened the door for my first date with Ken, I was surprised. Compared to my typical over six-foot, blond, physically imposing but mentally pliant choice in men, Ken was the opposite. Ken is about five feet seven inches tall with dark hair, olive skin, and a medium build. The hat and the boots he wore at the Halloween party made him at least five inches taller. He was by far the shortest man I ever dated.

Ken walked into my apartment as if he owned the place, said something funny, and took a seat on my couch before I offered. With one step into my house, Ken seemed less predictable, different from anyone I'd dated. Part Woody Allen, a dash of Bill Murray, a little streetwise Eddie Murphy, and a hint of a Texas drawl, his style confused me, sparked my curiosity. *Did Jews really live in Dallas?* Jews in western gear seemed an oxymoron to me.

I offered Ken a beer while I went to my bedroom to put on makeup. That's when he saw my journal. The journal sat on the coffee table, inadvertently left open. Ken sat on my couch, had a moment of conscious guilt, then picked up my journal and started to read:

> Something is changing—I feel a certain comfort, satisfaction, even preference of existing without a lover . . . I want to do more with my life than worry about men and work. I want to figure out a way to release all this pent up sexual energy without sleeping with anyone . . . .

Always the man with an unflinching poker face, Ken never mentioned what he read until years later, after we were married.

From the start, Ken made me laugh. He told jokes, spewed lines from *Caddyshack* and *Annie Hall* with perfect cadence. I liked his green eyes, the way he leaned forward when I spoke. There was something impish about him, high-voltage energy packaged in a calm exterior. I liked his confidence, the way he kissed, the way his hands read my body as though they couldn't wait to know more. I liked the way his mind worked, fast, sure, never fogged with second guesses.

At the same time, I counseled myself to keep my options open. Ken would finish Stanford in the spring; he'd probably move to another city. Three years younger than me, I doubted Ken considered marriage. I predicted we'd date until graduation, then drift apart. Years later, Ken told me he knew he'd marry me after our first date.

A friend at work alerted me that I'd struck potential financial gold with Ken. With degrees from Princeton and Stanford, and a two-year stint at Morgan Stanley, Ken would likely take a job grossing hundreds of thousands of dollars annually. The idea struck me as odd. I knew people who gained wealth through stock options and high risk, but the idea of a base salary exceeding $100,000 or $200,000 per year, not to mention bonuses, seemed extraordinary, slightly obscene.

"And, by the way," he said, "you might want to take that swastika off your neck. The cross might offend your hot-shot Jewish boyfriend."

Swastika? My cross? I fingered my neck. I wore the small, gold Maltese cross that my father brought home years ago from his trip to Italy. In any school photograph of me, from first grade through high school, my gold cross hangs from my neck, four limbs expanded like the petals of a flower. I never thought of that cross as German or Nazi inspired, but that night I took off my cross and hid it in my jewelry box. I couldn't throw the cross out—that cross was one of the few gifts my father gave me. Ken never mentioned the cross and didn't seem to notice its absence.

I flew to New York for a weekend with Ken in January while he interviewed with some of the Wall Street firms. We stayed at Le Parker Meridien, ordered hot chocolate, and snuggled in the soft, white sheets. He showed me his old haunts from when he worked in New York with Morgan Stanley after Princeton and before Stanford—Greenwich Village; One if by Land, Two if by Sea; Soho; and Rockefeller Center. Flying from San Francisco to New York for a weekend seemed crazy to me, excessive, extravagant, and indulgent. Fun.

Ken thought big, bigger than me, bigger than anyone I'd known intimately. He didn't come from money, but Ken wanted to play for high stakes in the business arena. Ken didn't have my Catholic guilt and sense of deadening responsibility that comes with excess cash. He enjoyed money and never felt shy about spending what he earned on himself. "Somebody's got to be rich, and it might as well be me," he told me as we sipped our Calvados from oversized snifters.

The idea intrigued me, aroused me, and allowed me to order from a menu with no prices. Ken operated in a world I knew only from movies and books. I never lusted for that world, but Ken put affluence at my fingertips. The silk of a rich life felt smooth, unfettered by the sharp edges of financial angst.

For someone who planned to be rich, Ken wasn't materialistic. Clothes didn't matter; he didn't pine over a specific Mercedes or Porsche, or dream of a Rolex watch. He wanted the experiences money could buy—exotic trips, the best seats at any sporting event, weekends in New York, and a penthouse suite. When Ken backpacked through Europe with an old girlfriend, they scraped by on $2,000 for two months. He never wanted to stay in a youth hostel again or order the cheapest item on a menu just to sit at an outdoor cafe. Ken wanted his desires to determine his actions, not the lack of cash in his wallet.

Ken talked more than any man I knew. I felt as though I'd uncorked a bottle that'd been stored for a long time on a back shelf. He told me about his family, his mother's temper, and how his father met his second wife at a stoplight. Ken hadn't seen his father in several years, even though his dad lived in Dallas and Ken had spent the summer there. Ken's parents divorced when he was eleven. As happens in many families, the divorced parents' antagonistic relationship created barriers. Ken's father ended up on the short end of the visitation stick. In the same breath, Ken mentioned he frequently visited his paternal grandparents, who also lived in Dallas.

I tried to visualize Ken's family tree with his two sisters, half-siblings, adopted half-siblings, and various rounds of marriages. Against this backdrop, my family looked like a Norman Rockwell painting. Ken said he survived his childhood and adolescence with a full schedule of after-school activities. When he got home at night, he'd lock himself in his bedroom with his homework, a liter of Diet Dr Pepper, his cat Mittens, and a phone to talk to his girlfriends.

Despite his parents' rocky divorce and his mother's outbursts, Ken still did all the things expected of a dutiful son. Mother's Day cards, birthday presents—he did these things with robotic precision, trained to avoid the explosion. Ken's behavior puzzled me. For a man who seemed so direct about everything else, his actions with his mother didn't match. I asked him why he went through the motions of a son with so little heart. Why not ditch the relationship entirely or make some attempt to remedy the situation?

"She's my mother," he said in response to my advice to abandon the relationship. As for mending the relationship, he laughed, and shook his head no. "Too much time, low chance of change."

Strange, in retrospect, that Ken's unfailing loyalty was the one thing that kept our marriage and me alive during the worst parts of my depression. Most men would've left me, overwhelmed by the hopeless alter-person who emerged from my body. The stubborn faithfulness I questioned in Ken with his mother proved to be the same quality that made him stick with me, even when I could give nothing in return.

As our relationship deepened, Ken's relationship with his mother and our religious differences were the two things that worried me most. Otherwise, Ken impressed me. He showed a sense of caring and integrity in the way he treated me and his friends, encased in a fun-loving, brilliant sense of humor. We enjoyed each other, reveled in our differences. His attraction to me seemed instinctive, all encompassing—his love rose from his skin.

After dating a few months, on a night when I made dinner, Ken snuck up from behind and threw his arms around my waist. My head rested against his shoulder. I felt his warmth radiate through his arms. I felt so safe, so loved—so content. The embrace reminded me of something, an odd déja vù, I couldn't place. Then, as he kissed me, I remembered.

My dream.

Ken was the man I couldn't see, the one who waited for me. I knew then if he proposed, I'd marry him.

Ken's graduation popped on my calendar too soon. I met Ken's mom and step-dad at the graduation ceremony. After Ken's stories about his mom, I expected much worse. Barbara appeared all sharp edges, with jet-black, salon-starched hair, dressed in brilliant red with manicured nails to match. Her behavior didn't match the costume. She was pleasant, curious, high-energy, and fun, not at all like the person Ken described. Barbara seemed so different from Ken's description that I wondered what was wrong with Ken. "She's not so bad," I whispered in Ken's ear. "Why are you so hard on her?" His jaw locked.

Ken left for Dallas that June—no ring, no promises, only a trip planned to Australia together in mid-July. I prepared for the relationship's demise. When we sat on the runway in Los Angeles, preparing for our sixteen-hour flight, my hopes rose. *Maybe he'll ask on the trip.* Ken shoved the last bag into the overhead and plopped into the seat next to me. He told me about an encounter he'd recently had with his grandparents where he told them I wasn't Jewish. *Talking to grandparents? Sounds like pending marriage to me!* When I asked their reaction, Ken burst my illusion. "We're just dating. Why would it matter?"

After a few days in Sydney, I thawed, but not much. We headed to Cairns to spend a few days on Green Island, a serene spot in the middle of the Great Barrier Reef. One afternoon, Ken and I snorkeled a few yards off the beach. He pointed to something frantically and then pushed a piece of laminated orange paper into my hands. I unrolled the sheet and read the words: "Julie, will you please marry me?"

I shot up out of the water. I coughed, sputtered, ocean water in my throat. "Is that a yes?" he asked eagerly, more vulnerable than I've ever seen him before or since. "Is that a yes?"

I hugged him. "Yes! Yes, of course."

We talked a long time about religion, our future children, and how we intended to raise them. I hadn't attended church regularly since Notre Dame, and I felt no strong allegiance to my religion of origin.

Ken considered himself Jew Lite, a cultural but not a religious Jew. Even so, crosses bothered him, and he felt he'd betray his heritage if he raised his children as Christians.

In some ways, Judaism more closely aligned with my beliefs than Christianity or Catholicism. Still, the idea of raising our children as Jews frightened me. I'd read Primo Levi, knew the atrocities committed against Jews throughout history. *What if that happened again? Why expose my children to the threat of anti-Semitism?*

I knew I wouldn't convert. I knew Ken wouldn't convert—that went without question. Conversion seemed an obliteration of my personal history. I worried in a purely Jewish household my history might also vanish, whether or not I converted. I wrote about this in my journal, concerned I might become an alien in my own home, unable to celebrate my childhood traditions and rejected by my own children.

I demanded a Christmas tree. Ken agreed. He offered to expose our children to both religions, fill their Sundays with hours of religious training. This seemed confusing to me, more than ridiculous. I agreed to raise our children as Jews, discounting the impact of over 500 masses, a Catholic university, and thirty years of family traditions. *All religions have merit; we just need to pick one.* My open view of religion allowed me to jettison my own.

As we flew home, Ken coached me on a proposal for Octel. "Ask them to fly you back and forth from Dallas every week and demand a $5,000 bonus if you do this until our wedding," he said. I laughed. *They'll never buy it! They won't spend that much money on me.* Nevertheless, I walked into a senior management meeting and demanded the package as though I expected them to agree. No one even flinched. I flew back and forth for nine months, until my project reached completion.

The management team at Octel handed me my bonus check and threw me a raucous farewell party. Ken smiled through all this. Ken knows when he sees an undervalued asset. This insight in discovering untapped potential is something at which Ken excels, but I thought the gift applied to stocks and companies, not people, especially not me. I never realized I undersold myself. With Ken's help, I began to see myself differently, speak out, act with more confidence—take more risks.

We exchanged our vows on the stone steps of the Monterey Bay Aquarium, under a chuppah, with a rabbi and a priest. My brother Patrick walked me down the aisle, my sister Eileen stood as a bridesmaid, with my four closest girlfriends by her side. They all dressed in a deep royal blue. I picked the color and let them choose the style. Teddy and Matt read from the New Testament and Kahlil Gibran.

I incorporated components of both religions in the ceremony and asked Father Tony, my uncle, to share oplatek with both of us. Father Tony held the white rectangle of oplatek high in the air, and I could hear the inward breath of every Jewish person in attendance. "This is a piece of unleavened bread," Tony said in a clear voice. He explained the custom of oplatek, an unconsecrated host, and how my father shared oplatek with us with good wishes for the upcoming year. The crowd exhaled.

We exchanged our vows, shed a tear about Dad's absence, and smashed a glass. We shouted, "Mazel tov!" In that moment, the religious boundaries disappeared.

Ken and I strode out of the ceremony and into the reception, beaming. Ken's grandmother, Nanny, grabbed my arm after the ceremony. "Your uncle, the priest," she said, "he's brilliant." *This is how religion should be,* I thought. *This is how it can be.*

13

The Fine Print of Motherhood

I lay on our carpet, exhausted, brain-bent, eyes pasted on my one-year-old son. Andrew stood with his back to me, palms pressed against the window. He gazed at the branches outside, arched in the breeze. The light from the window made his oversized ears transparent, the blue veins visible beneath his skin. His body swayed with the sounds he made. "Whish, whish." He turned.

"Meem?" Andrew's word for Mom, his me ever-present.

His face showed the wonder of each new piece of information.

"Meem!" Andrew's eyes begged for an answer.

"Wind," I whispered. "It's called wind."

He tilted his head for an instant, as though he rotated the word in his brain. Then he turned to where he started, his back to me, hands on the window. The trees bowed. "Whish, whish."

I watched in awe. Nothing else mattered.

Nothing else mattered until the day ended and my list of to-dos remained undone. Or someone asked, "What do you do?" Or a friend called from work and asked me how I filled my days. I stammered, unable to account for the hours of my life that evaporated before I noticed.

How did this happen? After Ken and I married, I moved from product marketing into sales. Within a year, I closed a major account worth millions of dollars. The success continued. A few months prior to Andrew's birth, I defined a marketing strategy and presented the ideas to Octel's top management. How did a woman like that become transfixed by one child's motion?

Before Andrew's birth, I planned to return to work, six weeks off at most. I never saw myself as a stay-at-home mom. When childless, I viewed mothers who chose this route as weak. Clearly they didn't have the right stuff to manage their lives. Being a mother brought a whole new perspective.

The endurance required for motherhood made my professional sales and marketing occupation look like kid stuff. My days as a mother held rewards that filled my soul but often slipped through my fingers. In my sales or marketing roles, I might encounter a few rough days or even years, fringed with slammed doors and offensive people. I persisted. Almost always, my focus earned rewards—promotions, luxurious trips, high pay, and accolades.

No one cheered my strength of character when Andrew peed in my face or when my breasts swelled so much that Ken called me Bessie. The rewards of motherhood were intangible and long-term. By the end of some days—a lot of days—I looked at my empty hands and wondered what the hell happened.

On the bad days, my purpose as a mother hid in the mist that clouded my brain—the boredom, the repetition, and the physical ache. No paycheck, no commission, no vacation, no social or intellectual stimulation, no review, no real training, but hours and hours of investment in a child who might or might not despise me by the time he went to college. Motherhood required more blind faith than I could possibly muster.

Some women thrive on the baby years, intoxicated by soft folds of skin and miniature fingers that probe every orifice on a mother's face. I felt that way too, in ten-minute increments. Then I needed air, and none existed. I loved my child, but he overwhelmed me. My journal says I came to the "dull realization that I'd done something irreversible."

Motherhood might be tiring for most, but I began to think I was the only one psychologically devastated by a baby. Was this postpartum depression? Probably. No one ever made that diagnosis, and I rarely talked about how I felt. My reactions seemed unhealthy to me, unfit for a good mother. So I did what I do best with unacceptable emotions. I buried them. As they bubbled up, I pretended they didn't exist.

Plus, at the time, my biological urge to breed and thirty-five years of life training collided in a crash that left my psyche scattered in small, irretrievable parts. My parents, from the beginning, never told me I couldn't do something "because I was a girl." That's a good thing, right? My teachers, most of them, encouraged me, painted images of president or corporate leader in my brain.

At Notre Dame, my favorite business professor said I had chutzpah, and I had to ask him what the word meant. "Spirit, guts, grit," he said. "The qualities that make a great leader." At Octel, the president of the company told me I could run the company someday, if I chose to do so. In a period of time when sexual harassment and barriers for women flourished, I had more than my fair share of cheerleaders.

So what went wrong? Why couldn't I have children, hire a nanny, and live up to all this highly forecasted potential?

The trade-offs between motherhood and a career are tough for most, but I found them impossible. I wanted the best of both, a smooth trick I've yet to see any woman master. My version of motherhood and my definition of a career faced each other in a stubborn game of chicken. Unable to compromise on either role, I quit my job. At the time, I viewed my choice as a personal failure, a lack of discipline deeply etched into my midlife bones.

My six-week leave expanded into six months until all my vacation, sabbatical, maternity, and sick pay vanished, right before the holidays. With a queasy feeling, I deposited that last check. Ken wasn't a miser. I didn't fear he'd question what I did, but the idea of asking him for money rankled me. I'd supported myself for over twelve years. Even though the State of Texas claimed his income half mine, I felt like a child asking for allowance. My dependency on him shifted our relationship into a pattern neither of us liked.

Even though Ken's business surged upward, he encouraged me to return to work. I was passive, silent at parties, short on ideas, taking back streets to avoid the highway. Without a paying job, Ken feared I'd lose my sense of self.

"Go back to work," he pleaded. "Even for a little while." He wanted his wife back, that bulldog who feared nothing.

I knew I'd never be the same person I was before Andrew's birth. My former edge and my intensity seemed overwrought in the shadow of motherhood. At the same time, I didn't like the person evolving from my skin—tired, financially dependent, and indecisive.

Depressed.

Hours passed with me on the floor, analyzing the carpet as Andrew played. *Can work help me regain a sense of balance? Maybe Ken is right.* I picked up the phone, made a few calls.

I tried consulting, and then I attempted a job Octel created for me. I was miserable. At work, I felt distracted, unglued—physically there but mentally absent. When I returned home, Andrew shunned me and ran to his nanny for comfort. While Ken was on a business trip, I called him babbling about Andrew, how I hadn't slept, about a nightmare that erupted when my eyes finally closed. I told him I planned to quit the job Octel had designed for me.

"Are you sure? Are you sure?" Ken paused. The loudspeaker announced his flight in the background. "I gotta go. Just don't hate me later, okay? Don't blame me for what happens." Ken sensed a wrong turn then but didn't know how to change course. The arc and depth of the turn caught us both by surprise.

I gave birth to my first suicidal thoughts nine months after my son first squirmed in my arms. April, an infant, spring, a time of rebirth, and a new mother seem an odd combination for a death wish. Perhaps in winter my inner landscape matched the outside world. By spring, I realized the world healed while I remained broken, uninspired by the sun's warm rays.

My Easter Sunday journal entry chronicled my brokenness, black pen on a white page:

> . . . thoughts about suicide for the first time last week. That's
> so crazy! My life is so full! I have a husband who loves me, a
> beautiful child. Yet somehow my life feels uncentered.

Thoughts about suicide with no explanation, no shock; I'd described ducks in the pond in greater detail. When I found the entry years later,

I was stunned. I had no recollection of being that depressed. Tired, yes. Confused, certainly. But I would've sworn I never experienced postpartum depression.

I never mentioned these thoughts to anyone, not to Ken, not to my mother the psychologist; I never picked up the phone book or asked a friend if she might know a counselor I could see for a few sessions. The thoughts shamed me. I'm surprised I even wrote them down.

In spite of my blues-ridden state, Ken decided we needed out of Dallas for the summer. Ken wanted a chance to relax, gain perspective, and figure out the next phase of his business. Ken and his East Coast partner felt a move like this might allow them to transform the business. They picked Santa Fe. I packed our bags with an optimism I hadn't felt in over a year.

After an eleven-hour ride with my one-year-old, my enthusiasm remained intact. We reached the house we'd rented, high on a bluff with views of the Sandia, Sangre de Cristo, and Jemez Mountains. Close to nightfall, I climbed to the roof.

A vast expanse of desert spread before me in all directions. Storms brewed in the distance, black sheets of rain and a crooked flash of light. The air felt pure and my lungs filled easily, despite the higher altitude.

Somehow the sky that displayed stars and storms simultaneously, the damp smell of rain, the tension of electricity in the air, rearranged my brain. My thoughts changed from "oh well" to "oh my." *Oh my God. How lucky am I to be alive, to see the earth?* Salvation by scenery? I know the cure sounds too fast, too incredible to be real. Although my problems and life stayed essentially the same, my depression lifted.

This good feeling lasted about a week, but I began to feel trapped again, as I looked out the window or from the roof at three sets of mountains; they remained in the distance, with me stuck inside with my toddler. Catch, blocks, and the inane, predictable beat of Big Bird's nasal tone caused a fire at the back of my neck, even though Andrew's head bobbed along in time. Finally I grabbed him, locked him in his car seat for a ride to the local camping gear store. "We're going hiking." Andrew smiled with his blanket crammed in his mouth.

I didn't call Ken. He and his partner had headed out earlier that morning. I knew a call to Ken would result in a long list of questions.

Where are you going? Who is your guide? How much water will you take? What about a map? Supplies? According to Ken's plan of life, parenthood, especially motherhood, required preparation, planning, and a backup plan.

In theory, I agreed with him. In practice, this version of motherhood choked the life out of me. I strolled into the store, slammed down my credit card for a baby backpack, and asked about a decent trail I could hike that afternoon.

The man behind the counter sported a goatee and a ponytail with flecks of blond around his temples. He looked maybe ten years older than me, judging by the lines on his face, but fit. He reached for Andrew, perched on my hip, mussed his hair as though he knew the child. "Whoa there, sister, let's get one that fits." He pulled down three different packs as I glanced impatiently at my watch. Nonplussed, he insisted I try each pack on while he placed Andrew in the pack for fit. Satisfied with one, he took my credit card.

As he rang up the purchase, I asked him where I could hike that afternoon. "You don't wanna hike in the afternoon." He tapped his pen on the counter. "Storms."

I snorted like a bull, not a sweet gasp of resignation. I was hiking a trail that day, rain or no rain, directions or no directions. He could help me or get the hell out of my way.

He must've sensed my desperation or conviction, I'm not sure which. Before I had a chance to respond, he acquiesced. "Okay, okay, there's a short hike not far from here, fairly low, you can't last long with a kid that age anyway."

He pulled a "Map of the Mountains of Santa Fe" from underneath the counter and pointed out the Chamisa Trail. "A little steep at first but a nice walk." He traced the line of the trail with his finger. As I thanked him and turned away, he yelled, "Hey, lady, at least take the map, will ya?"

"Sure." I pulled a few bills from my pocket. "Thanks."

Andrew and I sped out of town, toward the ski basin. I noticed a dirt area with a few parked cars on the left. I turned, parked the car.

I loaded the pack with snacks and water and hoisted Andrew on my back. The trail jutted upward. My thighs strained for the first quarter of a mile, but then the trail leveled to the nice walk the man described. Pine trees swayed. Dust rose from the rocky trail.

Andrew squirmed in the pack, arms outstretched, fingers pointing upward. "Meem! Whish! Whish!" I felt the wind brush across my face. The strands from my ponytail blew in my eyes. The wind swept through me, in me, my spirit exhaled in time with the sound. A low moan with no pain, the earth's Om.

"Yes, that's what we call wind, my sweet boy." I reached up, grabbed Andrew's hand to my lips, and kissed his fingertips. "We've found the wind again."

_14_

Stress and Self-Honesty

 he words tumbled out of my mouth before I landed on the couch in Dr. Yvonne's office. "I can't believe this. I had suicidal thoughts."

Dr. Yvonne looked worried. "Recently?"

"No, no, no." I took a deep breath. "About six months after Andrew was born."

"Oh!" Dr. Yvonne sank into her chair. "Much earlier than the attempts."

I did the math in my head. "Six years earlier."

Dr. Yvonne acquired her shaman look, a gaze in the distance where she summons those probing psychological questions. "And this bothers you. Tell me why."

"Why? Because I can't even remember! It's like—like suicidal blackout." I grabbed my hair at the roots and then realized how crazy I looked. I let go. "How can I do that?"

"How could you do that?" Dr. Yvonne squinted as if I should know the answer. "Think about how you've reacted in other situations."

"What do you mean?"

"Think about the doctor, at Bethesda. How long did you hold that in before you told anyone?"

I counted. "Probably six, maybe seven years."

"This seems the same habit." Dr. Yvonne took a sip of tea, mulling through the information we'd exchanged. "You seem to discount the impact of stress and the benefit of assistance." She put down her cup. "Six years is a long time to go without asking for help."

In the four years after Andrew's birth, I took my do-it-yourself parenting seriously. Just as I gained my footing with Andrew, a year after his birth, Ken lobbied for child number two. I hesitated, wondering if another child would plunge me back into the slush of exhaustion. Ken believed if we didn't have another child quickly, we might not ever have a second child. Ken methodically laid out all the points of his argument, persisted, and won. I acquiesced. After all, I wasn't working.

How could two children be that difficult? I figured I'd be pregnant when Andrew was two, and the children would be about three years apart. That age span felt comfortable, but my plans, as most plans involving children, didn't transpire as expected. I got pregnant the first time we had sex without birth control. Becka and Andrew were less than two years apart.

Almost a two-year gap exists in my journals after Becka's birth, the longest absence of writing in my life. With an infant and an energetic two-year-old, I barely had time to take a shower, much less write down my feelings.

That time period was exhausting but happy. I found a nanny/housekeeper, Abby, who cleaned efficiently and had a good sense of humor. The kids and I loved her. Andrew, endlessly curious, sparked my interest in life with his enthusiasm. Becka, a calm old soul in a newly born body, accompanied us on trips to the zoo, the Science Place, Discovery Zone, and various parks around Dallas. I don't remember any postpartum depression, but without my journals after Andrew's birth, I would've denied postpartum depression for that time period too.

Through a number of sessions, Dr. Yvonne and I examined the other stresses that piled up in the six years prior to my first suicide attempt. During that stress-building period, I served as a primary caretaker for my two children at the beginning of their lives and Ken's grandparents, who faced the end of their lives.

Nanny and Grandpa felt like the grandparents I never experienced; separated by geographic distance, my biological grandparents and I barely knew each other. Grandpa Hersh called me his Kosher Shiksa. Grandpa always counseled me, "You do too much, my Kosher Shiksa. You do too much." He was a sweet man, short, round, nearly blind, with a voracious appetite. He called himself the fat man.

We hired a helper for him when we took away his car keys, and I managed his helper. I paid her each week, outlined her responsibilities— driving, shopping, and minor cleaning—and brokered the disputes between them. Grandpa rarely complained, but Nanny had a new list of issues each week. "She used our phone, snapped at Grandpa, and put her soda on my grocery bill." Each week she'd sing a variation of the same theme. Grandpa missed his car but adapted. He'd sit at the Luby's cafeteria all day long, smoking his pipe, having conversations with the Mexican busboy who spoke no English.

Nanny reminded me of an older, Jewish version of my own mother. Sharp witted, sharp tongued, Nanny always sold the most tickets for the annual raffle at the Jewish Community Center. At eighty-five years of age, she'd go to Golden Acres a few times a month to "help the old people." She stood about four feet eight inches, and she could intimidate anyone. She'd stand at the fish counter at the grocery store as the fishmonger searched for her over the counter, only hearing her voice. "Is this fish fresh?" she tapped her finger on the glass. She encouraged me to go back to work to keep my sanity. "You do too much for other people," she said. "You're going to wear yourself out."

She'd say this, but then call me as if her house were on fire. "Target is having a 50 percent off sale on yarn today! Can you take me?" Nanny never learned to drive. She lived thirty minutes from our home. I'd change Andrew's diaper, throw him in a car seat, and race to her condo to help out. When I got pregnant with Becka, the process continued.

Soon I cared for two small children and two grandparents in their late eighties. As my children progressed, their great-grandparents regressed. In the same week Becka took her first step, on an April morning, in a field with bluebonnets, Grandpa got his first walker. Never in my life had I understood that the beginning and ending of life are painfully similar, filled with dependency. The idea rocked me, made me wonder about my own life.

On top of this, Ken's mother, Barbara, required her share of visits. In-laws—I suppose some life stresses are timeless. Barbara never complained about the time we spent with Nanny and Grandpa, the couple that sired her divorced husband whom she still despised. She simply expected equal time when I was already overextended.

Barbara seemed oblivious to my emotional and physical exhaustion. She demanded that we show up at social events where she was honored, with our children in tow. She wanted the photo-op, the image that she could be the brilliant career person and perfect mother, too. When I protested, Ken warned me, "Look, I've dealt with this woman for thirty-five years; it is easier to do what she asks than weather the outburst." Ken couldn't see that I was bursting on the inside. Neither could I.

Did I argue? No. I set boundaries as best I could, boundaries that had to be reset every year, every month, and every week because Barbara would ignore them. She'd claim cultural differences. "Remember that dinner scene in *Annie Hall?* The one with the Jews and the Christians? You just think differently than me."

I remembered that scene, Annie's WASP in-laws lifting their forks to mouths in silence, in a perfect ninety-degree angle. My dinner table looked nothing like that, but Barbara never asked. Cultural differences might have accounted for part of the problem, but personality type played a larger role. Barbara's indifference to my boundaries made my vulnerable psyche an easy mark.

The collision of different cultures in the same marriage produced a unique stress; Dallas is Ken's hometown, and Judaism his hometown religion. I don't really have a hometown—too many moves, too few attachments. Although I adapted to Dallas, my transition felt far from seamless, especially in a city where familiarity and appearance counts. I didn't grow up in Dallas, didn't know the streets, the families to know, what "Hook 'em Horns" or "Gig 'em, Aggies" meant, or which schools were better than others. I never had a pedicure until my mid-thirties and had a manicure only for special occasions. In Dallas, land of Botox and anatomically correct women, unpainted nails are the social equivalent of a sizable chuck of spinach lodged in one's front teeth.

Religion made a difference too. Not in terms of content, but context and culture. Whether I liked it or not, my Catholic characteristics couldn't be erased. Born and bred Catholic, I now lived in a Jewish world. I never converted, and although I learned the customs and enjoyed them, they didn't resonate with me in the way "Silent Night" or communion did. Over time this dissonance has subsided, as the music and traditions of the Jewish faith feel more familiar. But without the childhood connection to the traditions, I experienced an emptiness. Something was missing. Dallas Jew is not my native tongue, even if I'm fluent.

A change of financial state, an expensive mortgage, change in living conditions, and change in residence—all these stresses burgeoned when we moved into our new house in Dallas. Already uncertain of who I was and to which group I belonged, money became the final alienator.

"The house drew a spotlight on our wealth." I twisted on the couch in Dr. Yvonne's office, unable to find a comfortable spot. "Our friends, all with great jobs, still worried about bills and how to afford tuition." I rubbed my left palm with my right thumb. "Their problems felt more real than mine. Money made relationships awkward."

Dr. Yvonne adopted her shaman gaze. "Did *they* feel this way, or did you?"

I glanced out the window, aware of how the blind split the scene outside into small segments. "I'm not sure. I think it was only me, but I really don't know."

She nodded. "Understandable."

"Is it?" As one taught to worry about lack of money, the problems of an abundance of money felt ridiculously self-indulgent.

"We are individuals nurtured by community, Julie." She drew a deep breath. "When you moved, your small bit of solid ground vanished."

I thought about the day we moved from our 3,000-square-foot house in Irving to our 10,000-square-foot house in Dallas. We gave away almost all our furniture, certain our old trappings lacked the status required for our new home. I swallowed. Dr. Yvonne was right. My small bit of solid ground disappeared.

15

The Big House

I want to feel outside when I'm in." I spread my arms when I spoke, trying to convey the wide space of the outdoors.

The architect nodded and took a few notes. "I can see a wall of windows opening to the backyard. High ceilings, lots of light."

"Yes, yes!" I liked the creation phase of building a house, before the concrete forced so many concrete decisions. When the architect sketched the house, he sprinkled his own version of pixie dust on the page.

"What about the front of the house?" Ken stood and stretched. "I want a circular drive and a big gate."

"A gate? Do we really want a gate?" Didn't big fences alienate neighbors?

"Yes." Ken slid back into his chair. "And a billiard room. A movie room too."

"Do we really need our own movie room?" I already fought with the kids about watching too much TV. A shrine of a movie room sent a mixed signal.

"Yes." Ken pointed to the architect's notepad. "Write that down. We can afford it."

"A billiard room?" I shook my head. What next? Would we hide weapons and ask if Colonel Mustard did the deed with the candlestick?

"Live a little!" Ken grabbed my hand across the table. "We can finally do this."

Finally? I never lusted for a big house or a circular drive. At the same time, Ken seemed so excited. How could this be wrong?

As the house neared completion, pixie dust gave way to hundreds of small choices. Details. Costs. Alternatives. I squirmed as the questions began. *What do you want? What type of flooring? What stain of wood?* The questions continued on lighting, carpet, texture, color, granite, and marble. My head spun. *What did I know about finishing out a 10,000-square-foot house?*

We hired a designer, my stomach in knots. Style. Feel. Period. *How the hell do I know?* I drove a Nissan Sentra over 120,000 miles until the vinyl backseat disintegrated. What did I know about style? *Are you within budget?* I'd look at the numbers and feel sick. "Come on," the designer would plead. "Let's have some fun with this." Fun? For me, the process felt like strangulation, suffocation, *stuffication*. So much stuff needed to fill the empty space.

Six weeks before our move-in date, I mentioned to my friend Candace that we'd not selected any furniture. Candace thought the house was too large, overwrought for a young family with two small children. "Nine bathrooms? For four people?"

The furniture in our existing 3,000-square-foot house was a ragtag collection of Ken's black lacquer post-college items and my Santa Fe flavored white-washed wood. I planned to donate our old furniture to Goodwill. I ran into Candace at carpool. I leaned on her car as she advised me from her driver's seat.

I shrugged my shoulders. "How long can it take to find new furniture?"

"Months." Candace rolled her eyes. "It could take months."

"Months? Can't you buy this stuff at a showroom?"

Candace shook her head. "No, no, no, not for a house like this. Not the right scale."

"Scale?"

"Size, dimension, how can you build a house like this and have no idea about what goes inside?"

Good question. I must have been at the zoo that day, in the woods, or glitter painting with my kids.

Our kids didn't care about furniture; they could play hockey in the living room and bowl in the den. Ken wanted the house furnished, but he had other worries on his mind. Work heated up; deals needed his attention. "Just do it," he urged. "Try to be within budget, something lasting, in a timely manner, and in good taste." *Good taste?* I'd spent the last four years consumed with old people, potty training, and first steps. Good taste meant tastes good. Every empty room and blank wall screamed at my incompetence.

We were rich now—rich enough to buy anything we needed to give the appearance of wealth. Yet with each thing I purchased, I felt more uncomfortable, awkward, and an obvious fraud. At the same time, I felt I ought to be able to fill the house. After all, I wasn't working. I wanted to do a good job at something, please Ken, and make a home for my family. In good taste, of course. Panicked, I called friends, asked for references, and discovered Moranda.

Moranda agreed to meet in front of my new house, then in the final stages of construction. I ran that morning, took a shower, put on clean sweats and a T-shirt so I could take my kids to the park after school. Moranda drove up in her white Lexus, the gravel scattering under her tires. When she stepped out, her stylish brown boot peaked beneath the door. I stuffed my stray strands of hair into my baseball cap. *I'm writing the checks. It doesn't matter what I'm wearing.* She shook my hand; I apologized for my appearance.

"Oh, no worries." Moranda flicked back her white-blonde hair. I felt short, really short—my running shoes were no match for her three-inch heels. We chatted for a bit, traded names of acquaintances. Moranda explained her fee structure, which seemed reasonable. She was single, childless, in her mid-twenties, wanted more experience, a break into the high-end market. Ambitious and direct.

"Have you thought about the style you want?" Moranda's speech had been scrubbed for accent. I doubted she was from Texas, but unlike most people, her words gave me no clue of her origin.

"Style?" I knew what she meant, but hoped if I repeated the word, I might think of something. I dug my hand into the pocket of my sweats, felt a rectangular shape. I pulled out an old monorail ticket from the

Dallas Zoo. *Style? Tropical forest? Savannah? Savage Beast? Early Savage Beast?* Style. Why did I feel like I was shrinking?

"You know, more contemporary, French, or classic?" She held her chin up, as though she were thinking deep, stylish thoughts, tapping into the supreme universe of good taste.

"I like a lot of things—" Indecisive. Bad answer. Vague.

"Eclectic then, eclectic with some traditional accents." Interior-design speak for someone with no direction.

"I guess . . ."

"What pieces do you have from your old house?"

"Pieces?"

"Pieces, you know, furniture, art, what are you bringing here?"

I cleared my throat. "I have these batiks, from Africa, my brother Teddy sent—"

"African batiks," she interrupted. "Now *that's* eclectic." Then without a breath, "There'll be room for those upstairs, in the kids' area."

During our tour of the house, Moranda and I stepped into the dining room.

"I thought the batiks, maybe the dining room, might add some—"

"Oh no, a room like this—" Moranda stretched out her arms as she turned around, her heels slowly tapping on the wooden floor, "deserves more than that."

"You think so?" I said, not sure if I should be insulted or flattered.

"I know so."

Moranda led me to her car and handed me several issues of *Architectural Digest* and *Veranda*. She advised me to peruse them, get a feel for what I wanted. We agreed to meet the following week, at the Dallas Design Center, to look at fabrics. The wheels of her Lexus scattered gravel as she drove off.

The next day began at 5:30 with the jerk and push of life, a life that required quick answers. I yearned for a slice of day without interruption. I pulled on my running clothes, yanked my hair in a ponytail, and brushed my teeth at a speed and fury that suggested I'd overslept. A white-mint residue lingered at the corner of my mouth, erased with a splash of water and a rough dab of the towel.

With one glance in the mirror, I knew I looked worn, needing makeup I'd never apply, lacking those extra minutes of rest I never allowed myself. I straightened my shoulders and ran my tongue across my teeth. "Good enough," I whispered at an image that looked older than the self I imagined. *Good enough.*

In darkness, I felt my way to the nightstand, opened the drawer to grab my journal. Ken stirred, mumbled a question, then rolled to his side in a sound sleep. I tiptoed out of the room, down a hallway of windows, to see the sky painted in swaths of deep pink and orange. I paused in honor, then slid to the floor, cross-legged. I opened my journal. My pen scratched out the first sentence.

It's been a long time since I've written.

I heard a tap to my left, a footstep. Five-year-old Andrew descended the stairs in a slip-slide motion, with his right hand to his ear. His dark hair, tousled, fell across his face as he pushed his head to the side. He wore a white T-shirt with Rangers spelled in blue across his chest. The shirt flapped against his legs, well below his knees. Dark circles hung beneath his eyes.

"Mommy," he sniffed, "my ear hurts."

I sighed, closed my journal. Andrew crawled in my lap and leaned his head against my chest. "Poor boy." His body melted into mine.

The alarm sounded in our bedroom. I calculated the logistics of school, pediatrician's office, and a grocery run. The sky paled to a blue so faint the color blended in my mind with one of the trim colors the builder asked me to pick the day before—Antique White, Eggshell, Moonlight, Snow White. *Can't white be white?*

By 5:00 p.m. I rubbed my eyes, hoping to squish my vision into clarity. *Dinner. Something simple. Tacos. Need meat. Need cheese. Not that hard.*

I ached. After holding a sick child, a jealous healthy child, trying not to breathe infectious diseases in the pediatrician's office, three calls from Nanny, a Target run for yarn and PediaCare, hauling groceries, and three games of Candy Land, each small step felt legion.

The garage door creaked, signaling Ken's arrival. His step was light as he entered the house, not resembling the drag and pull of my own feet. I hated him. The hamburger in the pan turned from pink to brown. I remained at the stove with my back turned.

"Hey there." He leaned over my shoulder to kiss me. "How's Andrew's ear?"

"Better."

"Bad day?"

I shrugged. He moved behind me and rubbed my shoulders hard, too hard.

"Owww! That hurts!"

Ken flung his hands up in the air and shook his head. "What's with you?"

"Nothing, just tired."

He sat down at the table, grabbed a fork, and tapped it on the placemat. "You're always tired."

"*Always* tired?" I turned the burner low and swirled the taco mix and water with the beef. I felt beyond burnt, frazzled. Tired.

"Always. The kids first, then running, then your friends, then the cat. There's never anything left for me. Last man on the totem pole."

I squinted at him, not sure if he was making a joke. The line of his jaw, teeth clenched, let me know otherwise. I was stunned. *Why now? What did he expect from me?*

Tears burned at my eyes, but I turned my face away from him. "I can't give any more than I'm giving." I put my hand on his shoulder, but he jerked away.

"It's just been a long time since you surprised me."

His words stung, then became another stone in my pack of guilt as I trudged through the kitchen. I pulled the plate with the diced tomatoes, olives, shredded cheese, and lettuce from the refrigerator and set the food on the table. I turned away to get the meat from the stove.

Ken clutched my wrist and pulled me toward him. "Well?"

"I don't know what more I can do."

He dropped my wrist and pushed me away. "That's the problem."

Screams raged in my head. I wanted to list all the things I had done for him, but they were practical things, nothing special. I opened the refrigerator door, pretending to look for something.

I slammed the door shut. *Damn him!* I didn't expect him to surprise me, to cheer me on. Why did he need me? We were parents; the kids came first. Guilt and embarrassment crept at the corners of my anger. Ken did try to surprise me. He brought me gifts, flowers, not only for the obligatory birthday or Valentine's Day. And in return, I, well, I was tired. Always tired. My brain felt stuck in the gooey fluids of my day.

"Call the kids." I scooped the meat into the taco shells. "Dinner's getting cold." Every shell cracked when I filled them.

I felt so alone my first five years of motherhood despite being physically surrounded. Between Ken, Ken's grandparents, Ken's parents, and our own children, someone always had a request for me. No matter what I did, someone inevitably felt disappointed or wanted more. After a while, I was disappointed to be so disappointing. Because I knew the results in advance, the work got harder. I couldn't surprise anyone, including myself.

My friends helped me slog through this unanticipated hazing of motherhood, each one with her own sage wisdom and flaws. Miriam, Sarah, Tara, and Roxanne from the Shabbat group, and my newfound friends from St. Alcuin school, Candace and Kate, all faced their own flavor of challenges. Our circumstances were different, but we were universally overwhelmed. Moments with them—play dates, runs, walks, or stolen moments for lunch—spanned the loneliness, gave me a gulp of air as we laughed about our daily predicaments. But we were all busy, juggling young children, work, illness, and potty training while trying to carve out a life with our husbands.

We were all college educated, several with advanced degrees, all sapped by the delusion that we could do everything. Most of them learned more quickly than I did. Miriam pulled back; she was always the first to leave and the first to define limits of engagement. "Gotta go" became her call sign. Candace got sharp, hard. Roxanne used humor, and when that ran out, she'd explode or collapse. Kate exorcised her demons at the Cooper Center track. I ran faster, did more, took on volunteer projects, and filled my schedule instead of saying "no" to anyone.

When I'm busy, I can't think. I can't hear the water lapping on the edges of the all-too-private island I've created. There's a high to busyness, zipping pell-mell through life until the wall appears. I'm not sure if my tendency to do this is learned or genetic, but my father routinely overloaded his schedule, as did my brothers, my sister too. Workaholics, we arrive early and stay far later than our counterparts.

Most of the time, the busyness reaps great rewards. Organizations love the output, whether they are corporate, government, or volunteer. But sometimes, for some of us, the wall appears. Suddenly the blue sky turns eggshell white and our world shatters into bits we can't reassemble. My siblings seem to cope with the crash better than I do, some of them avoiding the wall altogether. When the wall hits, I find myself on my island, alone, exhausted, and poor company. As our house moved toward completion, foundation poured and framework set, while the floors were laid and fresh paint dried—I was in high flight, approaching the wall.

When we moved into our big, empty house, the rooms felt like the outside. Our house was overwhelming, an inspiration, an impressive edifice, but not a home.

Moranda assured me she could fill our house. I had my doubts. We had appointments to hit the Dallas Design Center, Donghia, Legacy Antiques, and George Cameron Nash—all the places one needs to make a house a home. All the essential accoutrements as dictated by Moranda's Law, quite different from Newton's, unlike the rules I'd learned from the forest, the Church, or forty years of movement from place to place. Moranda possessed an unwavering confidence in her own good taste.

As we walked into the first showroom, Moranda's tight silk skirt scraped against her legs with each step, making a sound like flint struck hard to ignite a flame. Edmund scurried out to greet her, grabbed her shoulders, and pulled her cheek next to his, kissing the air. "Stunning as always, my love." He brushed the invisible lint from her shoulder. Only Moranda could pull off three-inch spike heels, hot pink skirt, and flimsy white blouse with a deeply cut lace camisole underneath. If I wore clothes like Moranda's, my friends might ask if I planned to turn tricks or attend a costume party. But on Moranda, The Designer, the clothes fit.

Edmund and Moranda chatted for a few minutes while I eyed the tables and chairs on the floor. Thick wooden tables carved with intricate patterns, high-backed chairs padded and covered with fabrics etched with gold, and rich blues and reds filled space as far as I could see. Tall grandfather clocks with elaborate faces stood with time frozen at different points, none matching the digital display on my sports watch.

When my phone rang, Edmund pirouetted in my direction, eyes sharp on my Gap Classic Cut jeans. My phone showed Nanny's number. I hit "ignore call" and stuck my phone in my purse.

"And who is this?" Edmund's voice hit a different note with each word.

"Oh, I am so sorry." Moranda pressed her palm flat to her forehead. "This is Julie, my client."

Edmund extended his hand to touch my shoulder. He hesitated, pulled away, then clapped his hands together twice like a kindergarten teacher about to sing his favorite song to the class. "There's so much to see."

As Edmund turned on his heel and walked to the other side of the room, Moranda smirked, shot a conspiratorial glance at me, twittered her fingers, and tip-toed after him.

I stepped forward to follow them and a ray of light pierced the window, hitting my right eye, so bright I had to hold my hand to my face to block the stream. With one more step, the light faded. My eyes took a moment to adjust. They cleared to catch Edmund massaging a mosaic table with his right hand, telling Moranda this piece was just the thing I needed.

16

The Unexpected Outcome
of Anticipated Loss

*N*anny sat in an empty hallway in Presbyterian Hospital in an orange straight-backed chair. She clutched a large manila envelope in her hands. With her glasses off, chin jutted forward, she rubbed her eyes. Her legs, crossed at the ankles, swung beneath the silver legs of the chair.

She startled, then focused on me. "It's bad this time."

I sat down next to her. "What are you talking about?"

"The doctor's note, on the X-ray. He told me not to look, but I did. I have a right to know, you know."

I laughed. "Nanny, there's no way a doctor would write your death sentence and hand you the note." I held out my hand. "Let me see that."

I deciphered the radiologist's jumpy notes.

Female. Ninety years old. Remarkably strong muscular structure for age. Benign senescence of the spine. Slight osteoporosis.

"This isn't bad!"

"What do you mean? I've got senescence? Has anyone survived that?"

"Well, I don't know what senescence is, but benign means harmless, like a benign tumor."

"I've got cancer?" Nanny put her hand to her chest.

"No!"

"I knew it was bad," she said, shaking her head. "So senescence is some fancy word for cancer they made up."

"No. No! I don't know what it means."

Nanny shook her head. "Can't fool me."

I recounted Nanny's story with Ken's father, Bart. He chuckled at her fear of *senescence,* which he defined as a medical term for normal aging. Normal aging, I suppose no one does outlive that. He warned me about Nanny, told me she'd have me running to the doctor twice a week. But somehow, this event seemed different to me, prescient, predictive. The radiologist saw senescence, but Nanny felt the final outcome.

Grandpa passed away before Nanny did, before we moved into the big house. Luckily he maintained his health until the last six weeks of his life. His death had an impact on me, but I barely had time to pause. The move, my children, and Nanny consumed all my attention.

After we moved into the big house, Nanny's health slipped further. My children were four and six. Both of them had graduated to "lunch bunch" and stayed for a full school day. My roles had changed from builder, planner, and teacher to the solitary roles of chauffer and caretaker.

My kids, being older, were messier. They had friends, soccer games, and birthday parties on the weekends. The creative portion of my parenting role seemed over, sliced into hourly events, an empty shuttle between pick-up times. I tried to write but didn't have any stories worth telling. After all, who wants to know about piles of laundry, soccer games, and doctor visits with an aging grandparent. I felt guilty when I did try to write. *Wasted time. You'll never be a writer anyway. You have too much to do.*

I'd start the day with a plan, but the phone would ring with another request from Nanny. Plans changed. I adapted. *Nanny might die this year or in months.* If I grumbled to myself about this endless caretaker role or hinted that I might return to work, I felt selfish, arrogant. I knew the kids, Ken, and Nanny needed my care to keep their lives on track.

Nanny complained constantly of pain, and her sons, Bart and Stephen, had lined up a series of doctors for her to visit. I walked into her sitting room one afternoon, to see her hunched on her couch. Pillows bunched behind her head and her back, as she searched for that one position that might bring relief.

"I'm tired." She turned and winced. "I'm done with doctors."

I crouched on a small, padded stool, reached out, and rubbed her arm.

"The boys say I have to see all these doctors." Nanny faced me. She pushed her right fist against her back and grunted.

I stood up and placed a pillow behind her back. "Any better?"

"No." She shooed me away.

I plopped back on the stool. "Do you want to see the doctors?"

Nanny's eyebrows furrowed. "No."

"Then don't."

"But—"

I held up my hand. "Nanny, you are ninety-one years old; you can do what you want. You can see or not see doctors. You can eat or not eat. You can live or die."

"I'm ready to die." She looked out the window. "I miss him."

I nodded. I knew what she meant. She missed Grandpa.

"Don't let them put me in a home."

I nodded again.

Nanny deteriorated after that conversation. I felt as though I'd given her long-awaited permission to unwind the final strands of her life and make an exit. I visited her several times a week, usually when the kids went to school.

Nanny asked me to pull out the birthday cards she bought in advance for the upcoming year and help her sign and address the envelopes. She worried about her bills. She must have asked me about the Sears bill every time I visited; the account had been paid months earlier. An efficient woman, Nanny didn't want to die owing anything to anybody. Maybe if we'd kept an open balance at Sears, she would've willed herself to stay alive.

During one visit with Nanny, her eyes brightened and she sat up.

"Julie, is that you?" She strained to see me.

I touched her hand. "Yes, I'm here."

She lay on her gold couch in her sitting room, white matted hair resting on the arm. I crouched by her side. The light through the window came in slats from the venetian blinds, bright outside, an empty sidewalk, sprouts of green emerging from dry, brown grass.

"Hurts so bad."

I looked outside, wished the right words of comfort might be etched on that white sidewalk.

"The pain will be over soon. The bills are paid. Everyone is fine. We love you. I love you. It's time to go."

"I love you too." Her body trembled. She turned her head away from me.

"Hurts bad," she whispered to the back of the couch. "Worse than anything."

"I know, I know." I held her hand for a long time. Sounds filled the silence—the beep of a truck backing up, the dumpster's contents sliding with a crash, an upstairs neighbor's heels clicking as she ascended the stairs. Their lives continued, oblivious of this woman a few yards from them, hunched on a couch, mouth formed in an "O" like a bird, waiting. Waiting.

I visited a few times more after that, each time feeling heaviness in my chest as though her search for air had become my own. The doctor said he thought she might go on for days or weeks; he didn't know which. I shook when I heard that news. Her pending death stretched me, pulled at me, took me back to the weeks before my father's death. Each visit pressed with the weight of inescapable loss.

My dad died at age fifty-eight, and Nanny died at age ninety-one. Nanny's extra thirty-three years of life didn't bring her to a heightened level of spiritual consciousness that made her more prepared for death than my father, with his midlife interrupted by cancerous surprise. In terms of a life lived, a life content, she seemed less ready.

When my dad suffered through his last days, people from the church sat in shifts with him. His wife counseled him, and his children left work, traveling long distances to be with him. With Nanny, we did what we could and hired help to fill the rest. Everyone visited, but we all knew the game. Nanny haggled for her next visit within fifteen minutes of our arrival. Her constant need for more time from us wore us down, wore me down, anyway. We all seemed ready for Nanny to die, almost impatient.

Nanny survived, her pantry stocked for the next disaster. She always chided as we left her apartment, "Close the gate. Close the gate." No loose ends for Nanny.

My father lived the way he danced, fluid, as though by instinct, but he clearly had been taught the steps. She always asked, never got enough. He rarely asked for anything and always had more than he needed.

As I watched Nanny die, I wondered what my own death would be like. My life looked so different from my father's. No Catholic Church, no struggles for income, no students, and no garden I'd tended. Could I die as he did when I refused the steps that fit him so well? His steps never fit me, I knew that, but I still wondered. *When I die, will someone miss the sound of my voice?*

Finally, one morning, I held Nanny's hand and talked with her for a long while. I watched her breaths slip in and out.

"Nanny, I know you can hear me. This is the last time I will see you in this body." I read her Whitman's "Song of Myself," stanza six. The part about the green sprouts showing there is no death. That death is luckier than we all imagined.

If Nanny could hear me, her body didn't react. I felt compelled to speak. I had a knack for one-way conversations with unconscious individuals.

"The bills are paid. I love you. The next time we meet, we meet in a different place."

I kissed her on the forehead, walked out, and slammed the gate shut. *Close the gate. Close the gate,* I heard her voice as if she spoke.

She died about four hours later.

Four hours, the same amount of time my dad died after my last conversation with him. The timing unnerved me. Did I pull a last psychological plug before their brains went flat? I called Candace, asked her to pick up my children. I told her if she ever needed to die, I'd be happy to send her off.

"Stop talking." Her cell phone cut in and out. "You're scaring me."

I drove to White Rock Lake, sat on a bench, and wrote a poem—the first one I'd written in a long time. Nanny's most sage piece of advice, "It is what it is," fills the last stanza. The water lapped at the edge as I sketched the words, by myself, without my brothers to help me finish this funeral poem. I had no plan for Nanny's service. Tired, always tired, I closed my eyes but could not rest.

17

Adrenaline Escape

Ken's uncle put his hand on my shoulder. "Could you write her obituary?"

I nodded. I felt honored, part of the tribe.

"Great. The deadline for the morning paper is in an hour."

"What?" I glanced at my watch. "There's no way."

Ken's uncle explained that Jews don't embalm their dead, so funerals must happen within a few days of death. "Do the best you can." He jotted down the time and location and handed me the note. "People need to know about the service."

I stared at the scrap of paper in my hand. Nanny lived ninety-one years. Her life was summed up by me, her granddaughter-in-law, the Kosher Shiksa, in fifteen minutes.

After a short service, we buried Nanny next to Grandpa. A canopy shaded the open grave. The lowering mechanism creaked until her coffin hit bottom. Ken's uncle took a shovel and dug into a pile of dirt. The brown earth landed. Thud.

The rest of the family followed: Ken, his father, his aunt, his cousins, and friends of the family. Thud, thud, thud. The Mourner's Kaddish, chanted in Hebrew, wound through shovel strikes. Jews bury their own dead, a hands-on culture, physically close to the bitter end. Ken's cousin handed me the shovel. Tears filled her eyes, but mine remained clear. The blade bit earth.

Compared to my father's funeral, Nanny's burial lacked pageantry. She had no caisson drawn by black horses, no words of resurrection. No one snapped a flag into sharp corners. Soldiers lowered my father in the ground at a distance, while we drove away. My brother saluted Dad's grave in his dress blues. We let strangers fill my father's grave.

Nanny's funeral brought death close. Nanny lived. She died. Dust to dust. As a born and raised Catholic, I recognized the familiar tune, but it gave no comfort. Nothing softened the loss. My poem for Nanny remained silent, the words too trivial to be read aloud. Whitman's sixth stanza felt abstract. Green sprouts didn't spring from the brown rectangle of her grave. My hours with Nanny disappeared, the result of my efforts intangible. Days, months, and years of my time seeped into the ground.

I felt numb. I didn't hurt, so I assumed no wound existed. My schedule filled with joyless tasks, without a clear purpose. Many people reach a critical point in their lives when mortality becomes real and the need for a purpose in life more focused. Some turn to their family for nourishment, some to religion, and some to alcohol or harder stuff. Some hide out in their homes with candles and soft music. A healthy person recognizes a need to heal and allows time, space, and support for healing. However, in my numbness, I didn't see a need for comfort. I trudged forward, aimless. With a genetic predisposition for depression, an open wound left me in a perilous state.

In Nanny's death, I saw a life without luck; a life I feared had become my own. When I thought about the next fifty years of my life, I felt saddled. The chores mounted: house care, childcare, eldercare of my mother, my mother's death, care of Ken's parents, their deaths, then the care of my own husband. These life tasks stretched like a long corridor of hospital rooms with no windows.

Ken has psoriatic arthritis. His knuckles swelled. He hobbled out of bed in the morning, thirty-eight years old, unable to lift his arm higher than his shoulder. Ken eventually found a combination of drugs that allowed him full movement with minimal pain, but at the time, relief eluded him. He was irritable, pessimistic, with one repeated theme: "When I get old, you'll have to push me in a wheelchair." I felt responsible for him and tried to humor him. At the same time, I envisioned years trapped on cruise ships and in card games, when my legs could still scale mountains. I loved Ken, but squirmed under the weight of our future.

Nanny's death drew a spotlight on the unseen, the gap felt, but at the same time untouchable. "A spiritual vacuum," I wrote in my journal. Aware of my role as caretaker, the glue that held others' dreams, I felt dreamless, without energy to recall my own passions. When I did my best work, my glue dried invisible. Others' lives flowed with my transparent effort.

I prayed for an inspired life. I lit candles, sat cross-legged on my office floor, and opened my palms to receive divine guidance. In a brief meditation, a thought blossomed: the selfless life is the key. I didn't feel up to the task. The selfless life appeared a long, dull haul, with no relief. I wanted the woods, joy, and the unexpected. I wanted to have some core of myself left. The Selfless Life. The phrase alone left me tired, yet unable to sleep.

While I meditated with palms open, *Forbes* magazine featured Ken in an article. We were on different tracks. Ken's route created more wealth, more recognition, more events to attend, and more possessions. He reveled in his business success. I was happy for Ken but felt as if I'd become the caretaker for his spoils. I was the one who dealt with his children, his laundry, his mother, and the giant house of his dreams while he traveled and made brilliant decisions. I felt overshadowed. I wanted to be more than Ken Hersh's wife or the mother of Ken Hersh's children.

In an effort to shake my numbness, I sought peak experiences. Extreme behavior caused an adrenaline rush, which I labeled happiness. One day I took my children and two of their friends to the Dallas World Aquarium, all of them under six years of age. First, we fed the penguins. Andrew's buddy leaned far over the fenced boundary, toward the water. With his brows clenched in concentration, he pummeled the curator with questions. "What's the nicest animal in the world?" "Why are penguins black and white?" "Why do they like water?"

The curator ignored him.

Undeterred, the boy marched over to the woman and tapped her on the shoulder. More questions.

I laughed and encouraged his vivaciousness. I set no boundaries.

Once we exhausted her, we raced to the jellyfish tank, then the shark area. Then we stormed the machine that squished our pennies in the shape of four different aquatic animals. Satisfied, we sought our next event.

Four lanes of traffic, four children, and one childish adult, we held hands and screamed as we sprinted across the street. We passed the fire station, to Fountain Place, where a tiered fountain structure lay beneath I.M. Pei's triangular masterpiece in downtown Dallas.

In the summer, water surges from these fountains in tall and short bursts, periodically soaring, then vanishing from sight. Becka, Andrew, and I created an aquatic tag game on a previous visit. The game finished with wet clothes.

We wanted to show our friends this game but found the fountains off. A workman noticed my arms flying up and down to demonstrate the rise and fall of the water, and he accommodated me—he turned the water on. The children raced against the fountain's pulse. Soaking wet, we walked back toward the car.

I noticed a fire truck pulling into the station. We stopped. I asked for a tour, and four firemen appeared to lift the children onto the trucks. Andrew's friend readied his questions. "Why are fire engines red?" "Where is your spotted dog?" "Can I wear your hat?"

Finally, we crossed back over the four lanes of traffic and jumped into the car. Everybody in? Great! Buckle up. Becka's four-year-old buddy buckled her belt and sighed, "Can we do this again tomorrow?"

My friends paled with exhaustion from stories of an adventure like this, with a series of questions I never thought to ask. "Four kids under six by yourself? What if one ran off? How did you cross the street? Wet clothes? Are you nuts?"

The adrenaline sustained me for days, high on these chance combinations that jelled. Magic. But the everyday tasks of life cratered me—Andrew's earache, clutter in the house, a plan for dinner, or a family photograph.

Care of the house weighed like an unshakable anchor. One day I cleaned the house in a dead sprint, mopped floors, wiped down the kitchen, swabbed all nine bathrooms, and vacuumed what seemed miles and miles of carpet. Exhausted, I fell asleep midafternoon. I hired a cleaning service, which helped, but those women speed-cleaned and left. We didn't cooperate or form a team. They cleaned. I wrote the check. When they were in my house, I felt like I shouldn't be there.

The scale of routine home maintenance matched our square footage. In the past, when light bulbs burned out, electronics broke, or windows needed to be washed, I fixed them. I sprayed the Windex and wiped. If a light bulb needed a change, I scaled a ladder and swapped old for new. With a twenty-five-foot ceiling, changing a light bulb or washing a window becomes a different task. Our house required appointments, specialists, routine schedules, attention to detail, and bulldog persistence to see projects to completion. I didn't really ever *do* anything; I simply made calls and waited for others to do the work. Once again, my efforts felt transparent. My time didn't produce anything tangible but evaporated in management. Time spent on a dream house that had never appeared in my dreams.

We employed many people to keep up our house, which seems like a good thing, but for many years I felt like a stranger in my own house. There was always a guy in my yard: the landscape guy, the pool guy, or the guy to fix the latest thing that broke. Some of the people who worked for me seemed more at home than I did. They knew where things were and took pride in the small touches they made to my house.

They worked so hard I felt as if I ought to be doing something, but I didn't need to do anything. My kids were at school until 2:45 p.m. The house was built, the furniture installed, and the phone no longer rang with Nanny's requests. Nothing to do. That sounds like a dream, doesn't it? No need to earn a cent or lift a finger. But this wasn't the life I'd dreamed about. I'd worked all my life. I liked projects, work—a sense of purpose. I didn't know how to be a queen with servants.

With all this free time, I figured I'd start writing, but the words got stuck. The landscape crew watched me stare at my blank computer screen through my floor-to-ceiling windows. My broken Spanish didn't allow for conversation. I wanted to tell them my father came from a family of thirteen children. My father's family shared one bathroom. My grandfather worked on the Chrysler assembly line. My father spoke Polish when he started first grade. Two generations ago, our families didn't look that different.

I wanted them to know I wasn't like the women who lived in houses like this, even though these women now called me and invited me to this luncheon or that dinner to raise money for the "underprivileged." I wanted my landscape crew to know, but I didn't know enough words in Spanish to defend my expenditures, to differentiate my wealth from theirs.

Instead, I'd go to the luncheon and try to make conversation with former members of "The League" as they wrote checks, traded stories about old times, and admired each other's shoes. That's how they said it, "The League," as if anyone worth anything was once a member and everyone ought to know the organization. Too embarrassed to ask, I finally uncovered the missing word weeks later. "Junior." The Junior League.

One night Ken and I attended a dinner for board members of St. Mark's school, Ken's alma mater. We entered the Crescent, a prestigious office building in Dallas, and wove through the crowd to the patio. A waiter offered a glass of white wine on a rounded tray. My fingers wrapped around the elegant stem. I took a long sip.

Ken shot a hard glance. "Go easy."

I breathed out.

Ken spotted a fellow board member and turned toward him. I sipped my wine and slipped into the background. Snippets of Ken's talk drifted over the chatter of the party: "President Bush . . . Colin Powell . . . Rainwater." The fellow board member begged for more detail. Ken elaborated. I took another sip.

The women in the party all seemed cut from the same Dallas cloth—tall, straight blonde hair, dressed in slimming black. Perfect bodies, long legs. They kissed each other's cheeks when they met. One approached me. I stuck out my hand.

She looked amused but shook my hand. "You're Ken's wife, right? Let me introduce you." The names floated past me. They resumed their talk of charities, teachers, the weather, and books.

One of them turned toward me. "Have you read anything good lately?"

I hadn't read a book in months. "No, not really." I'd only driven carpool, cared for kids, and waited for repairmen.

She tried again. What did I like to do? Did I volunteer anywhere?

Why did she want to talk with me? I didn't want to talk to me. The chimes rang to let us know dinner was served.

She smiled and sat elsewhere, far from me. The waiter filled my glass. He looked past me, on to the next person. I cut my chicken breast into shreds, unable to eat.

After enduring a few of these events, I encouraged Ken to go by himself. Ken would return home from dabbling with the movers and shakers of Dallas to his wife, who conversed with small children all day, hadn't showered, yet maintained an essence of Clorox. Lemon scented but Clorox.

My weight dropped; people complimented me on the lost pounds. Ignoring the only other times in my life when I'd obtained pencil-thin status—when I contracted pneumonia and when I was depressed at Notre Dame—the weight loss seemed a good thing. I had dark moods, but with enough projects or peak experiences, they dissipated.

One of these projects was a flip off the diving board. I catapulted myself off our diving board, time after time as Andrew, age five, watched my back redden with attempts. Andrew marched to the board. "Mom, it's like this." He took three steps, spiraled forward in a perfect ball, and entered the water feet first, the first time he tried. He made the flip look so effortless, so easy, like his father's psychic business moves, like the spread of my father's arms off the high dive. "You just see it," my son advised. "Then you do it." I visualized. I practiced, again and again. Andrew sat at the edge of the pool, frustrated, ready for a new game.

Ken was worried. For the first time since he knew me, I had no appetite. He'd suggest a new restaurant, and I'd beg to stay home. He tried to humor me, lighten my mood, but I remained rigid, overwhelmed with my projects. Undeterred, Ken suggested a girls' trip for my fortieth birthday. After much prodding, I agreed. My birthday celebration evolved into a rafting trip down the Green River in Utah.

In late May on the Green River, I felt like the Grand Marshal of Extreme Luck. Coincidences conspired, but secretly I felt the incidents revolved around my presence. A last-minute cancellation of another group left our group of eight alone with three women guides. We lowered our raft into the river in an unusually warm May to find the river almost empty. The sun toasted our backs as we paddled, all wearing our "Unruly with Julie" baseball caps Ken gave us before our trip.

Three of us celebrated our fortieth birthdays—our cake thick with chocolate icing. Miriam, her divorce filed but not final, stayed long, danced on the beach in the moonlight, her steps light in the shadow of the fire. My friends from different phases of my life bonded, laughed, and made commitments to a new life—less work, more living, more peak moments like our days on the river.

For the first time in my life among friends, I felt crucial, the hub of the wheel, not a wayward spoke. I flipped off the front of the raft, into the frigid water, in a form even Andrew would have applauded. I felt lucky. I was lucky to be alive, to be able to afford a trip like this, and to have friends who could celebrate with me.

The high continued through the summer in Santa Fe as my conviction in my own luck tested the boundaries of safety. Most of the time, the high exerted itself in simple overscheduling. I'd start the day with a sunrise run up Fort Marcy Hill, through the plaza, up Canyon Road, down roads I'd never crossed before or checked on a map. I liked that panic of disorientation, the minutes where I'd run four or five miles and realize I had no idea where I was. Fighting my thirst and the ache in my legs, I'd look for signs, tops of buildings, mountains until I oriented myself.

My small risks eventually led to larger risks, as I required more adrenaline to obtain a peak feeling. In Santa Fe I gave a drunk man, a complete stranger, a ride home from the baseball game with my children in the car. I *felt* the situation was safe. When he proved harmless, my faith in my luck redoubled. I felt connected with the spirit world, protected by a full-time staff of guardian angels, unhindered by restrictions of common sense.

I forced my children, ages four and six, to hike to the top of Atalaya Trail, 5.5 miles, a climb of 1,581 feet, with no other adult. I carried them when they cried to stop or when Becka got a bloody nose. About an eighth of a mile from the peak, both children sat on the ground and refused to move. I threw Becka in the pack, climbed to the top. Dropping her near the cliff, I warned her to keep still. I retrieved Andrew via a piggy-back ride. I told my four-year-old to sit still on a mountain, while I retrieved her brother.

Why?

My journal only offers this explanation: "but we were so close!"

What did I expect when I reached that barren slab of rock at the top of Atalaya? Divine intervention? A mystical experience? I wanted my children to be awed by the Jemez Mountains in the distance, the winding dirt road beneath us, and the drop from the cliff that we peered over while I held their hands.

None of the above transpired.

I'd forgotten why I loved the woods in the first place. My hikes in childhood rarely used a fixed trail. I cut my own path.

Exploration and discovery gave birth to inspiration. A forced march to a barren rock does not inspire, no matter how striking the view. Andrew and Becka both backed away from the rock as soon as we reached the top, exhausted, angry, intent on the path that led home.

When we returned to Dallas late in August, highs and lows repeated in more rapid succession.

One morning I sat cross-legged on my office floor and lit a candle. I opened my palms. In a trance-like state, I saw electricity enter the top of my head and my hands. Thin strands of white light, five or six strands at a time, that twisted and crackled as they shot into the core of my body. The light transformed me, charged me for the day.

Later that day, I ran errands, fielded phone calls, and juggled the family schedule from my driver's seat. A phone call cratered me.

Ken wanted a family photograph. His mother bought the session with the photographer as a gift. Ken had pestered me about this photograph for months, but I delayed. The photographer called and instructed me on the clothes to wear. I'd envisioned a casual shot, done in simple clothing. The photographer disagreed.

"You must be in something that matches."

I swallowed hard. Many of my friends had photos of their families in matching clothes, but the idea of my family, tidy in a rectangle, made me feel sick. "No, that's not what I want."

"You want casual? Not recommended."

Did I ask her for her advice? No. "That's what I want."

"Okay then, all khaki pants and white shirts. Make sure they're pressed."

"That's not what—"

"I've got another call. See you Saturday at ten."

I called Ken in hysterics. He was baffled. Why did I care so much about a photograph? What was wrong with me? Why did matching clothes unglue me? He didn't ask much of me; why couldn't I complete one small request?

By the end of the conversation, I felt crazy.

His questions rattled in my own head, louder than any defense I could muster. I hung up the phone. The photograph felt false to me, hypocritical, but my reaction seemed overwrought, even to me. I felt the gap, the unseen void. Unable to define the feeling, unwilling to ask for help, I fell deeper.

18

The Inaugural Attempt

Ken flipped between CNN, Fox News, and NBC. Ken was a news and political junkie, and election night ignited him like some high speed freak making a score. He swiveled in his burgundy leather chair at a pace that made me nervous. "This is history. This is history." His eyes darted toward the screen. "We might know the next president of the United States."

I curled in a ball on the couch next to Ken's desk and stared at the inlaid gold of his fireplace mantel.

"Let's go to the inauguration." He shook his head. "I'll go. I'll go by myself. I know you hate those things."

I shifted on the couch. "I'll think about it." My face turned away from the TV.

Well after midnight I went to bed, the votes for Bush and Gore still unsettled. Ken's arm pointed toward the screen's glowing embrace, the remote molded to his hand.

Nearly four months and thousands of examined chads later, I stepped through the lobby of the hotel in Washington, D.C., worried about my outfit for the first inaugural event.

Our politically centrist gang—Ken, Candace and her husband, Doug, Miriam, and I—headed toward a reception featuring former

President George H.W. Bush. With the exception of Candace, none of us plastered stickers on our cars or lined up evenly with the Republican platform. Candace's politics slammed hard right, and she made no apologies. She often accused me of being a closet Democrat, not buying my best-person-for-the-job-or-the-time rhetoric. Her husband, Doug, kept his mouth shut.

Despite our different political views, all of us felt hopeful in this change of administration. Bush had pulled Democrat and Republican Texans together; maybe he could pull the country together. The women dazzled each other with their new outfits. Ken straightened his black bow tie, and Doug fiddled with his cuff links. Miriam glided in her black gown, her glass held high as she toasted to a new era of peace and compromise.

At the reception, we weaved through a mass of dark, wet coats and a lone mink. People stomped their feet, shook their umbrellas, and entered the round hall. The fifty-foot decorative oil rig in the center of the floor, surrounded by a bale of hay and a teetering wooden fence, collided with any image of what I thought might be presidential. The people looked the part. Women sparkled in gowns of emerald, lavender, and silver that swept the ground. Men stood attentively in their tuxedos.

Everybody wanted to be seen with somebody famous. Even famous people hunted other celebrities. Flashbulbs burned my eyes from all sides. The party felt like a political *People* magazine in live form, every person caught on film, summed with a caption.

Ken and Candace thrilled in the frenzy. "Oh look! There's Bill O'Reilly!" Ken rushed toward O'Reilly while handing Candace his camera. I wanted to remind Ken how much he hated Bill O'Reilly, what a dolt he thought the man was. Too late. Ken shook Bill's hand while Candace snapped. At the bar, I gulped a glass of chardonnay.

Retreating to the upper balcony, I watched the mayhem from a safe place. In a few minutes, Ken found me, frantic. "Bush Senior is coming. You've got to shake his hand." He dragged me down the stairs and pushed me up to the velvet rope where Bush Senior would pass. I resisted, but Ken shoved his palm in my back. "He knows me. You don't want to miss him."

My head spun from the wine and the mass of bodies around me, all clamoring for the touch of a former president. To me, the captivation with fame seemed absurd. Why did I have to touch him? I felt no desire to fondle an appendage. As Bush Senior approached and extended his hand to mine, a woman dove over my body and snatched his hand. "Oh, Mr. President!" In a second, Bush Senior passed. I turned to Ken, who beamed like a proud father.

"You shook his hand?"

"No."

"What?"

"Some woman tackled me. Look, I don't care."

"What? This may happen only once."

Ken pushed me again, with such force that I found myself on the other side of the receiving line rope. Ken ducked under the rope and pulled me behind the stage where Bush Senior had given his address to the crowd. We stepped over thick wires and made our way around the other side of the stage. We were now ahead of Bush Senior but on the wrong side of the rope.

"There." Ken brushed lint off his tux. "Now you can shake his hand."

"Are you nuts?"

"No, you want to shake his hand, and now you can."

"Ken, I want out of here. You care about this, not me."

"Why did you come?"

"I thought I might miss something."

"You're not going to ruin my experience."

I eyed my route for escape. "I will not dive over people to shake his hand."

Ken spotted Bush Senior, about twenty yards to our right and approaching fast. "Suit yourself." Ken ducked back under the rope and disappeared. I moved back, farther behind the stage until Bush Senior passed. The crowd thinned.

Furtively, I edged from the stage area in a beeline toward the bar. "Another white wine, please."

Drink in hand, I climbed the stairs to the balcony. From there, the bulbs flashed at a comfortable distance, the bodies rubbed, and smiles rose and fell as though in a movie, some disconnected scene I watched from my perch.

Miriam found me, elbows on the balcony, my glass held like a sacred chalice. "Amazing, isn't it?"

"Sure is." I wondered if she felt the same way I did. *Why does everything seem so fake to me?* My reaction to the inauguration felt extreme, a repeat of my hysteria about the family photograph. I shook my head, smiled, and steeled myself against my proclivity for terminal seriousness. *No one likes a judgmental bore.*

Miriam studied my face. "You look tired." She leaned against the balcony. "Are you okay?"

"Fine, fine," I lied.

When I watched President Bush's face on the JumboTron at the Texas inaugural ball, he looked tired, a little uncertain. In the distance, we watched him spin a step or two with Laura, crammed shoulder-to-shoulder with thousands of cheering Republicans. *How strange their lives will be from this point on.* Life on a JumboTron, connected with everyone and no one in the same instant.

When we returned to Dallas, gray webbed the sky like a mat. A soggy December preceded that month, followed by an even darker February, precipitation higher than any other winter since 1944, fifty-seven years earlier. The weather reminded me of my freshman year at Notre Dame, the same perpetual gray that left me desperate for a hint of blue sky.

I hadn't slept well the week before the inauguration or during, something I wrote off to pretrip jitters and the slant of an unfamiliar bed. But even back in my routine, I found no relief. Becka got sick, and Andrew battled nightmares, all requiring taps on my shoulder somewhere between the hours of 1:00 a.m. and 3:00 a.m.

I got sick.

"There is nothing physically wrong with you." My doctor adjusted his white coat. "We all have bad days. We have to force ourselves to keep going."

Spring erupted, flowers bloomed, and my depression lingered, my mind gray despite the clear weather. I was hopeful on that first day of

March, after my first appointment with psychologist Artie Raymer. I visualized myself leaping off the edge of a raft into ice-cold water.

I slept that night, but nine days later the handwriting in my journal jumped, and I made a strange admission after a long list of things that might be on anyone's list: "the kids need new clothes, garage must be cleaned, no recipe for dinner." The last item sits there on a page alone, as if I almost forgot, without a period at the sentence's end: "I think about killing myself at least three times a week"

I tried to assemble a photo album for Ken's birthday. Normally, photo books inspire me. I have photos of my family organized in albums, by year, from our wedding in 1990 to the present. Usually, I can pull from these albums and summarize a decade or two in a few pages of photos linked with words. The creation takes a day or two and my office looks like a wrecking ball hit when I'm finished.

The process and the result usually set my mind on a buzz for days. But with Ken's album, every page hurt. Every choice of word or photo felt immense. Worst of all, when I finished, I hated the result. Ken did so much for me, had organized one of the high points of my life—my fortieth birthday river trip.

In return, I copied photos and scratched some words on a page. *How can I ever give back to him as much as he gives me?* My personal deficit with him seemed insurmountable.

I began to forget things—names, meetings, and urgent phone calls. I mixed things up, put Andrew's lunch into Becka's lunch bag, lost my keys and my credit card, and forgot where I parked my car. All of these things might have happened before but never in unison, never was I so reliably unreliable.

My projects and tasks dropped: an auction project, room mother tasks, practices for soccer, and calls to parents on the team to let them know the game was canceled due to rain. Things didn't drop through the cracks but through ravines. My thinking blurred so badly, I wondered if I had a brain tumor or if I'd had a stroke.

My sister Eileen called me frequently. She recognized the warning signs. Eileen suffered from depression during college and through her twenties. I knew about her experience, but for the first time we talked in depth. Her severe downward swing presented differently than mine—she gained weight versus lost, slept more versus less, but the nervousness, exhaustion, and the overwhelming self-doubt matched.

I listened to her voice, staring out the window of my home office. Eileen reminded me of my accomplishments and promised the return of my former self. I wondered. *Did I see myself honestly then or now?* By mid-March, the old self seemed like an illusion, a mask finally torn from my face.

Mom called me often, told me to pray and prayed for me. She'd listen and offer advice, a counselor unable to unravel the mystery of her own child. I prayed too but got no answers. Instead of electric current, God felt nonexistent, in extended blackout.

Friends helped or tried to help, but I withdrew. I backed out of the book club, not able to focus on words, forgetting one sentence as the next one was read. Close friends noticed that in a year, I'd changed from the person who could put a positive spin on anything to a person who saw only dead ends.

For the first time in my life, I could say "no" to everything. No Shabbat group—our collection of twelve families that worked like relatives. No school projects. No volunteer work. I even avoided running with Kate at the Cooper Center. My evaporation, done quietly, slipped by most people unnoticed.

Stubborn local friends forced me to walk with them, talk with them, and eat lunch. But they had their own lives, complicated and time-consuming. More importantly, I let them see only a fraction of what happened in my head. I never told them about my lust for kitchen knives or that I stood on Becka's balcony and wondered how I could land head first.

One friend, exasperated, told me to give in to my depression. Perhaps a lesson waited for me in my depression's bleak embrace. The advice, which I took, proved perilous. I plunged deeper. She watched my words stop. She watched me curl into a ball and shake in my bed, unable to crawl out.

Life went on despite my soul stoppage. We planned to go to Punta Mita, a Four Seasons resort near Puerto Vallarta, for spring break. The task of packing loomed large. I agonized. *How many T-shirts? Bathing suits? What clothes for dinner?* Paralyzed with my notepad, I felt as if I were splitting atoms or telepathically channeling the cure for cancer.

I spoke to my sister-in-law, Paula, about how I felt for the first time. "Get to a doctor, now. Do not pass go." Paula knew the signs. "Get an antidepressant." My doctor was on vacation, but he prescribed a low-dosage antidepressant. He made me promise to come see him after our trip.

I filled the prescription and took the first pill. I was ashamed, humiliated that I needed drugs to prop me up for such an easy life. I didn't need to work. I didn't need to worry. In my mind, that formed a strange translation that made the knives and Clorox all the more inviting—I didn't need to do anything.

You are not needed.

When we arrived at the Four Seasons in Punta Mita, I realized I forgot to pack T-shirts for Andrew. Ken shrugged his shoulders and told me to buy new ones, at the gift shop, a hundred yards from our room. I felt my chest tighten. *The gift shop?* I'd never been there. *Can I find it?*

The room seemed so dark, the light outside blinding. I struggled for oxygen. I'd maneuvered through strange airports and cities by myself, but that spring a walk to the gift shop posed a greater threat. The room blurred.

Part of me saw this as ridiculous, high drama before I'd even seen the prices, but a larger part quaked. My legs shook. I felt cold despite the heat.

Ken looked puzzled. "Are you okay?"

"Fine, fine," I lied.

When I stepped out of our room, I panicked—afraid I would get lost, sure someone would see how crazy I was and lock me up. At the first turn, I stopped, noted the buildings, the trees, and repeated the room number again and again so I would not forget. 1000, 1000, 1000. Step, step, step. I pulled open the gift shop door. My hands trembled as I agonized over the price, the choice between the orange shirt with the sun or the purple with a starfish. Sure I had made the wrong choice, I laid the orange shirt on the counter.

"1000," I told the saleswoman, avoiding her eyes when she smiled.

"Buenos dias."

I returned to the room, shut the door, and turned the lock, out of breath. Ken had left a note. "Down at the beach, come find us—xxooxx."

I huddled on the floor for an hour. Could I find the beach and focus long enough to recognize their faces in a crowd? *Deep breaths, calm yourself.*

Determined, I pulled hard on the door.

Thunk.

The sunlight beamed in while the door caught hard on the chain lock. I'd locked myself in. I panicked, rattled. *Shit, what is happening to me?* I leaned my head against the door and closed my eyes.

When I calmed, I looked at my watch. Thirty minutes had passed. Time lengthened and shortened as if I skipped back and forth between invisible time zones. After lifting the chain lock, I reached for the doorknob and turned the knob again as if I expected a hurricane, a thunderstorm, an epic flood. The door eased open, and Andrew and Becka appeared before me, wet, feet dancing.

"Mommy, come play with us!" They chimed in unison. "We're at the pool. Daddy sent us to find you."

When I returned to Dallas, my symptoms worsened. Artie, my psychologist, agreed I needed medication. Artie recommended a psychiatrist who wrote me five different prescriptions. I still didn't sleep through the night.

I had nightmares, one where my friend Karen Sanders from high school asked me if I were still a Christian. Yes. Suddenly she had a tether on my ankle. She swung me cowboy style above her head and she repeated her mantra, "Then you must accept Jesus Christ as your savior." This dream occurred more than once. I'd wake each time, drenched in sweat.

I dreamed of a plane crash. When we hit, the water was warm, soothing. I stripped off my clothes and swam toward shore. I could see a group of naked people in front of me on a beach, basking in the sun. Behind me, near the plane, a group thrashed in their clothes.

Later, I set pen to journal to understand my dream. "God, what is the message?" The pen inked the following advice: "What you fear most will be your salvation, and you will survive."

Despite that consolation, survival seemed doubtful. Through April my journal goes in jumps and spurts: slept, didn't sleep, bad day, worse day. I wondered if I had an undiscovered learning disability.

Ken hired Margaret to help with the kids, the laundry, and house management—everything I had dropped. In her early fifties, Margaret dressed well, applying her makeup and styling her thick red hair with grace. When repairmen came, they often mistook her for the homeowner and me for the hired help. Even though Margaret treated me with care and compassion, I felt displaced. Her fragrance lingered on my sheets, on Andrew's and Becka's clothes, and made my skin itch. *Are they my children if they smell like her?* Stripped from each surface, my presence faded, scrubbed until invisible.

My close friends watched me, all on full alert. Tara and Miriam from the Shabbat group called me, cajoled me, and invited me to dinner. Kate insisted I run with her, despite my snail's pace. Candace listened and assured me I wasn't crazy. Elissa and Kristi—friends from my high-tech days in California—e-mailed. My sister called. My mother called. My husband looked worn. My children no longer tapped my shoulder in the middle of the night. They went to Ken. They knew I could no longer help them.

With so many friends eager to help and a new nanny, my children found a host of substitute mothers. *You are not needed,* the voice in my head taunted. *They're better off without you.*

In April, I wrote that I was feeling better—"the first night I could really relax."

The next page, undated, is a suicide note.

That morning, dressed in a white terrycloth robe, I gathered my supplies: the knife, notepad, and pen. The dew from the grass soaked my bare feet as I walked past our pool, past the waterfall that glistened over the boulders, to the backside of the cabana, the spot where we'd served snow cones the August before at our annual party. A bright day, clear sky—in another time I might have planned a hike, a long run, or a trip to see the meerkats. Instead, I huddled on the cement, pushed back the arms of my robe, and steadied my pen.

Thank you for all . . . but I have traded away too much and
now I am not certain about anything anymore.

So the note begins. I address my husband, my children, my mother,
siblings, and a few close friends.

. . . I no longer know who I am . . . Ken, as much as you love
me, I cannot figure out who I am around you.

The right arm of the robe dropped, dragged against the blue lines
on the page as I wrote.

So I am leaving so that you can figure out how to raise the
kids on your own. I trust your judgment better than mine.
Good-bye. I love you. You could not have done anything
more for me.

The note written, I took a deep breath and held out my wrist. Then
the argument broke out in my head.

Do you know what you're doing?

Well, no, I . . . I shook my head. The sunlight caught the dips of
the serrated blade.

Who's going to clean up after this?

I don't know.

*How long does it take to bleed to death, do you know that? Won't
someone find you first?*

I don't . . .

*Don't you have to be in water to keep the blood flowing? Won't your
blood clot? You'll just have the scars. Everyone will know you tried. And
screwed up.*

The blade rested on my skin, but I couldn't apply force, couldn't
silence the arguments long enough to cut. I stared at the knife.

Ken found me, eyes fixed on the knife, pen and notebook discarded.
His eyes moved from fear, to anger, to pain, to shame in less time than
it took me to drop the knife. My actions hurt him. My attempt to
take my own life hurt him in a way no apology or promise or passage
of time could completely mend. In an instant, our relationship had
irrevocably changed.

19

The Psychiatric Ward

Ken wasted no time, his patience shot. Like a good husband, he gave me an early birthday present that April, my first trip to the locked psychiatric ward at Zale Lipshy. A nurse showed me to my room, Ken by my side.

"My name's LaTisha." Fine red lines spidered through the whites of the nurse's eyes. "Let's check for sharps."

"Sharps?" My suitcase lay closed on the bed.

"Glass, razors, cords," LaTisha softened her efficient tone. "You know, anything you might use to do the deed."

Ken glanced away while I stared at my feet, unable to speak.

"It's okay, hon." LaTisha's long cornrows swung while she moved. "It ain't gonna happen here, not on my watch." She pointed to my bag. "Let's open her up."

I unzipped my suitcase. A framed photo of Ken sat on top of my clothes.

LaTisha gently picked up the frame. "That's a nice shot of you there," she nodded at Ken, "but you can't have this glass." She slid the glass out of the frame with practiced speed. She lifted my overnight kit, pulled out my razor, my toe nail scissors, and all my medications.

She pointed toward my feet. "I need your laces too."

"Shoelaces?" *From my running shoes?*

153

"You'd be surprised what people do."

After Ken left, LaTisha took my vital signs and weight, and asked me questions from a sheet that requested a response from zero (never) to four (always). Difficulty sleeping. Four. Sleep too much. Zero. Weight gain or loss in the last two weeks. Three. Difficulty concentrating. Four. Low interest in fun activities. Four. Lack of sex drive. Three. Feeling of hopelessness. Four. Thoughts of death. Four. Plan for suicide. I paused for a moment. ***Did*** *I have a plan, or* ***do*** *I have a plan?* I had a plan that did not work. Let's make that two.

The Hamilton Depression Inventory. A multiple-choice snapshot of mental health, neatly compressed on one page, a good diagnostic tool if the patient answers honestly. I did, the first time.

After the mental health quiz, LaTisha encouraged me to eat lunch. I sat next to a plump woman with frosted pink lipstick.

Another woman sat across from us. Her skin had deep lines, too much Texas sun. Her black hair twisted in a braid that dropped below her waist. Flecks of gray spiraled about her temples. When she glanced at me, her clear blue eyes summed my presence like the questionnaire I'd just completed.

"I'm Diana." She tilted her forehead across the table. "She's Betty."

Betty had been there for four or five days; she couldn't remember exactly. Betty had a cherubic face, someone I might expect to find at the public library reading books to children.

Between bites of her food, Betty told us her story. She'd tried a long list of antidepressants, but nothing seemed to work.

Diana listened to Betty's saga with me, churning her potatoes left, then right, with no forkfuls lifted to her mouth. "Has your doctor tried the ECT?"

Betty shook her head as her broad face flushed. "Oh, no. Oh, no."

"Betty, Betty. You just have to trust these doctors."

I set my sandwich on the plate, only one bite in the wheat bread triangle.

"ECT?" I swallowed. "What's that?"

"Electric Cleaning." Diana squinted one eye in concentration. "No, electroconvulsive therapy, that's it."

"Convulsive? As in convulsions? How do they do that?"

"Oh, it's not bad. They put you out. They hook these electrodes to both sides of your head and flip a switch." Diana put her hands on either side of her head and blinked her eyes. "Zip. Things get better. Right away."

Betty, now ashen, picked up her tray and waddled away from us without a good-bye. I wanted to escape but felt glued by Diana's stare.

I pushed my tray away. "Have you done ECT?"

"No, no." Diana held her hands out, palms up. "I'm just here until my meds settle."

I took a sip of water, my hands trembling.

Diana looked me over. "So what are you?"

"Me?" My mother often asked new acquaintances about their ancestry, so I knew the answer. "Half Irish, half Polish."

Diana's brow furrowed. "What?"

"What?"

"What diagnosis?" She exhaled in disgust. "You know, manic-depressive, obsessive-compulsive, anorexic, what are you?"

My therapy never got that clinical. In my sessions with Artie, he lit a candle and offered me a Fresca from his fridge. Our conversations centered on my mother, my husband, and me—a creative person without a creative outlet, he once said. Now this, ECT, a locked ward, a label required for processing. I glanced at my hands in my lap. "I don't really know."

"You will," she nodded. "You will soon. They name you, and it sticks."

After lunch, an intern named Jasper took me for some memory tests, a medical exam, and an EKG. At my insistence, we did an MRI for a brain tumor. Our insurance wouldn't cover the cost, but we paid anyway. A good friend of ours, a neurologist and a member of our Shabbat group, read the MRI after Ken and I pleaded with him. I prayed for a brain tumor. A tumor made sense. The confusion, the forgetfulness, I imagined a mass in my brain the size of a baseball, to which we'd all point and agree—no wonder!

I could fight a tumor but not something as invisible as depression, not a cancer without cells. Our friend smiled when he told me the good news, a completely clear scan, no signs of any problem.

I returned to my room, closed the door, no lock available to seal my privacy. "No locks in case I missed a sharp," LaTisha told me, "in case we need to stop you."

I lay in my bed that night, while a man raged in the hall. "What the fuck! What the fuck! They can't make me."

I'd seen him earlier in the day, planted near the community phone. The phone rang, and he yanked the receiver and answered with, "Yeah?" He was fat but strong, biceps bigger than my thighs, with eyes that bulged. Angry for a list of reasons so different from my list.

"What the fuck! What the fuck!"

I shuddered in my bed, my eyes clamped shut. The woman in the room next to me cackled, long and high, the lost, crazy sister of the Wicked Witch of the West.

The next morning, six of us gathered in a small room for "group"— group therapy. Charlotte led group in a lopsided circle of plastic straight-backed chairs. Charlotte's suit gapped at the buttons, her legs erupting from her knee-length skirt. When she talked, her lips glistened.

"Okay, let's begin." Charlotte placed her first transparency on a rickety projector that beamed THINK POSITIVE against the wall. The image tilted; grainy images clung to the wall, out of focus.

Gladys, one of the group members, popped out of her chair and began to pace back and forth. The back of her gown gaped, her white waist-high undies visible with each step. Charlotte urged Gladys to sit still, which she did for a few seconds, then hopped up again. Frustrated, Charlotte clicked off the machine, moved toward Gladys, guiding her toward a seat. Again, Gladys sprang to her feet, as if propelled by some magnet the rest of us couldn't see.

"Let 'er walk," Roby barked. Roby looked like an aged rock star, voice scratchy from too many cigarettes. "She ain't hurtin' no one."

Charlotte gave up and took a seat in the circle.

"Perhaps we should introduce ourselves."

The man to my right, Jack, looked like someone from my mom's side of the family. Irish. Fair skin. White hair. He sounded like them, that New York edge. He could have been some long-lost uncle my mother forgot to mention. He knew things were bad when he repeatedly peed in the closet.

"It stinks." The jowls sagged in Jack's face.

Charlotte nodded, leaned forward, elbows on her knees, her chin balanced on her palm. "Yes, yes," she sighed, "it's hard. I know."

"The carpet . . . ," Jack grumbled, "the carpet stinks like a cat."

Charlotte straightened, asked the next person for her story. A twenty-two-year-old woman showed her arms. She cut herself. The dough-boyish thirty-year-old, Joe, advised her to use a red marker across her wrist instead. Gladys paced.

Gladys paced the ten-foot diameter of our circle as the next person, Roby, relayed his tale. Gladys moved back and forth, back and forth. With Roby in midsentence, she glared at us. "I've got no reason to be here, no reason. No reason to be depressed."

"Gladys," Charlotte interrupted, "it's not your turn. Roby's speaking."

Gladys spun in Charlotte's direction. "Who's my doctor?"

The other patients ran through the list. Who's she got, Johnson? Cleaver? Weissmann?

"It's Johnson, I think," Roby offered. The other patients confirmed.

"ECT—did they do it?" Gladys looked from face to face. "Did they do it? They told me they'd do it."

"Yes, yes," the girl who loved her knife said, "I talked to you this morning, before you went in."

"Who's my doctor?" Gladys's eyes squinted, as if she could not focus on the voices.

The session ended soon after that. I went back to my room, shut the door, grabbed my pen, and wrote. My room felt familiar, as if I'd escaped to my childhood yellow room, shut the closet door, and lit the bulb above my head. In my new room, fear reigned.

"I have now spent twenty-four hours at Zale Lipshy," I wrote. An hour later, LaTisha insisted I leave my square, go to the community room, and interact with some of the other patients. I closed my journal, zipped it in my suitcase beneath my bed.

"Come on now, girl." LaTisha stood in my doorway. "You got lunch in an hour. Go do something." LaTisha, my new mother with cornrows, a gold-rimmed tooth, brown eyes versus blue, ousted me from my room to make friends with the other children.

In the community room, Joe, the dough-boy from group, sat across from a frail woman who stared at ten cards laid face up on the table. Joe, dressed in a red floral shirt and thick glasses, introduced me to Annie, the woman hunched over the cards, inviting me to join the game.

"Spades." He swiped the cards into a single pile. "Ever play it?"

My friend Karen Sanders and I played spades and hearts at the public swimming pool every day for at least three consecutive summers, but that was twenty-five years prior.

Joe refreshed my memory on the rules, and he dealt for three. Annie, gray, shrunken, looked as though her bones might snap as she gathered her cards. She shook, more frightened than I felt.

A round black woman barreled up to the table the moment we collected our cards.

"Joe, my man, is it spades?" Desarae mussed Joe's hair with a familiarity that suggested more than the four hours since she strolled in that morning. She plopped in the seat next to me. Desarae radiated so much energy I wanted to touch her, suck her mocha brown skin into my transparent white. Desarae pounded her fist on the table. "Deal me in."

Joe reshuffled the cards, dealt for four. While I struggled with which cards had been played versus those in my hand, Desarae whipped us. Annie's cards fell, some left, some right. Her frail hands trembled. I tried to help her. Two rounds into the game Annie quit, content to watch the slaughter.

Desarae showed no mercy, her ham-like biceps flailing as she laughed. "You got no chance, girl." She stuck her finger in my chest. "We are taught this game from the crib!"

I played and played, for the first time in my life in a game with no concern about the outcome. I wanted to be Desarae. I wanted to laugh like that, wild and certain of my own strength.

The next morning after group, I headed straight to the community room, hoping for a game of hearts. Desarae sat in the same chair she had the day before but didn't react when I sat across from her, pulled out the cards, and shuffled. "Hey, Des, do you know hearts?"

Desarae stared past me.

Joe wandered in. He touched Desarae's arm, snapped his fingers in front of her nose. She blinked like a drunk and leaned on the table to steady herself.

"Jesus." Joe scratched his neck. "They must be working on her meds."

I felt vomit creep up my throat. I swallowed. "They've killed her," I whispered, "broken her."

"No, Julie." Joe put a hand on my shoulder. "Some people come around in a day or two and they're completely normal."

I pushed his hand away. "Normal. Right, Joe. What the hell is that?"

"Out of here." Joe waved his right arm as if to lead me. "No knives, no head firsts off the balcony."

I wished I'd kept my damn mouth shut in group. He used my words against me.

"Alive," he finished.

"Alive?" I motioned with an open palm toward Desarae, exhibit one. "Is this alive, Joe? Really? At some point, aren't we better off dead?"

Joe shook his head. "Disorientation is temporary. Part of the process."

Desarae, medicated, had no reaction, a ghost in mocha skin where a hurricane once lived. I'm getting out, I thought. Today. No later. If they can break Desarae, I'd exit on a leash—someone's drooling but well-behaved pet. I pushed back my chair, walked away from the table.

"Hey," Joe yelled after me, "where are you going?"

"Out of here. Now."

"Come on, Julie, you just got here, they won't let you out yet!"

"Watch me, Joe," I mumbled the final words with my back turned toward him. "Miracle cure."

I did some good acting. Within forty-eight hours of arrival I swore my answers on the one-page Hamilton Depression Inventory had reversed—no longer suicidal, sleeping well, miraculously able to concentrate. I'd been healed, a slap on the forehead.

All lies.

The door to the fourth floor of Zale Lipshy unlocked. I made my exit.

20

The Cavalry Arrives

The light from our oversized windows flooded the bedroom. I huddled in bed, long after the alarm, a few hours since Ken took the kids to school.

My friend Miriam brushed the hair out of my eyes with her slender fingers.

I turned away. "G-g-g-go back to s-s-sleep."

"Oh no." Miriam had called me from work and decided a drive-by visit was necessary. "Time for a shower. It's almost 10:30. A shower always helps."

She helped me from bed as though I were an old woman, frail, bent, joints unyielding. "A shower and then food."

The shower helped. Movement helped. By the time I put on my clothes, Miriam had a bowl of soup and crackers waiting on my kitchen table.

"Eat." She handed me the spoon. "I can only sit with you for an hour, and then I have to go back to work. Roxanne's coming over a little later."

"You don't need to babysit me."

Miriam laughed. "Then stop sleeping until noon. Start eating." She raised one brow. "It's a plot, actually. I'm trying to fatten you up."

Miriam brushed the crumbs from the placemat where she sat. "Can you tell me how you feel? What you feel?"

I stirred the vegetables in my soup. "I haven't felt happy in a long time . . ." I put the spoon down. "Haven't felt anything."

Miriam nodded. She let the silence be, unaltered, in a way few friends in my life, few people in my life, could possibly stand. When I finished my soup, she hugged me and held my face in her hands.

"Look at me," she demanded. My glazed eyes met hers, so intense, so eager to solve the puzzle. "You have to believe this will change."

I didn't. I wondered if Miriam would marry Ken if I killed myself— make a whole family out of two broken halves.

Miriam glanced at her watch. "Look, I hate to do this, but I've gotta go."

"Gotta go," I smiled. Miriam held life together when her marriage crumbled. She set boundaries. She kept life in compartments that made life livable. Like my mother, like Ken. She could help my kids.

"Your children need you," she said as she walked to the door, waved good-bye. *Yes,* I thought, *my children need you.*

Miriam must have sent out the Shabbat group alert when she left my house because within ten minutes my doorbell rang. Tara entered, her voice in a constant upbeat lilt, her hair blown in a thick black tangle from her drive with windows open. "Ohmigod, it's so hot! Not even May yet! Let's go have a bagel!" Tara spoke in exclamation points. Tara lived between exclamation points.

A pediatrician, a mother, a stepmother, Tara juggled more balls more effectively than anyone I'd ever met. She dragged me to Einstein Bros. Bagels. We chatted about Zale Lipshy for a minute or two.

Tara drank from her bottle of water. "So, help me understand." She toyed with the bottle's lid. "Why did they let you out?"

"I felt better." Inadvertently, I set the fuse.

Tara's temples pulsed. "Wait a minute—one day you write a suicide note, and the next you're cured?"

The situation sounded ridiculous, but I didn't want to race back, lock myself behind the door to the psychiatric ward.

"Well, I told them I felt better."

Tara steadied herself. Breathed in, breathed out. "Do you really feel better?"

I thought for a moment but knew Tara would blow through any lie in a fraction of a second. "No."

"So Zale Lipshy isn't right. Don't you need to be somewhere? Someplace safe?"

I bristled, pushed back my chair. "Safe, meaning people will drug me? Make me chant some self-help mumbo-jumbo I don't believe?"

"Safe, meaning you won't kill yourself," Tara snapped.

I winced.

I could think about suicide, the how, the when, but when a good friend threw the act of suicide back in my face, I hurt. *Don't you dare,* Tara signaled. *Don't you dare kill yourself because I will kick the shit out of you.* Most people danced around the words, dipped and swayed. Tara swung and hit.

We drove home in silence. By the time we reached my house, Roxanne's car zoomed in beside us, sitter number three, the Shabbat group in full force. I expected to open my refrigerator and see a month's worth of premade meals. Our Shabbat group brings food whatever the occasion—birth of a child, bris, bar or bat mitzvah, wedding, milestone birthday, illness, or funeral. Food is the celebration, food is the cure, in the same way my Irish Catholic culture reaches for a drink.

Our Shabbat group takes problems by storm; they took my problem by storm—a combination of brainpower and energy to Shock and Awe my crisis into submission. I felt surrounded.

At the time, their unbounded affection seemed like interference, a distraction from my love affair with sharp objects and steep drops. *Why can't they let me be?*

They were too smart. They knew the fissure my death would cause in their lives, the guilt of a life lost because of that one thing they failed to mention. They knew the questions their children would ask, the fear, and the permission one violent act might give to someone else.

When we got back to my house, Roxanne leapt from her car.

"Can anyone buy me a drink in this joint? I want to hear about rooms in the loony bin." She swallowed me in a hug. "In case I need to visit."

Tara chuckled and drove off.

163

Normally, Roxanne makes me laugh. I connive time with her, I imagine ways our lives might intersect more so I can hear her latest near-death, dieting, social disgrace, or motherhood disaster told with unmatched, self-effacing hilarity. Her melodious voice glides through a story from crescendo to slapstick silence, yet tears well in her eyes when she reaches a soft spot. She's warm. A listener and a talker, she takes the stage and leaves with the adept instinct of a seasoned artist.

I blocked her entrance to my house.

"Look, Rox, you don't need to be here. I'm fine."

"You're not going to invite me in? Come on! I'll be hurt!" She put her hand on the door and pushed it wider, easing me into the house with the door. "You don't want to piss me off, you know."

"Rox, you don't have to sit with me. I'm not—"

"Who's sitting? As far as I can see we're stuck at the door."

"Not a child. You don't have time for this."

Roxanne had two children at the time, and I knew this visit with me interfered with a long list of items on a never-ending to-do list. Roxanne made time. She put her hands on my shoulders, pulled my face next to hers, nose to nose. "Right now, I've got no place else to be."

I backed away.

"Pretend I'm not here." She stepped past me, into the house. "Do what you'd normally do. I've got time."

Frustrated, I picked up my journal and walked to the back porch. Roxanne followed. We planted ourselves in two uncomfortable teak chairs that overlooked the backyard.

While I picked up my pen and scribbled, Roxanne opened her copy of *House of Sand and Fog*. Minutes passed. A mockingbird sang from a nearby tree as though its lungs might burst. Our lawn stretched green to the back fence, the winter rye in a lush carpet. The water cascaded down the boulders to our pool, which reflected the pure blue sky. In this oasis, my heart raced, my brain felt vacant.

Roxanne plunked her book on the table with a thud. "You know what bugs me most about this whole thing?"

I blinked, not sure if her book took a plot turn or she meant something else.

"I just don't get it." She pulled her long hair behind her ear. "As bad as any one day might be, isn't there any hope that things will get better?"

"No." Plot turn or not, I knew my answer to that question.

"Well, then, forget it." Situations that might leave an ordinary person agape get a perfectly articulated response from Roxanne. She tried another tactic, well practiced among Catholics, FARCs (Fallen Away Roman Catholics), and Jews. "Shouldn't you at least live for your children?" Guilt. Guilt works. Guilt always works. Roxanne knew that bait.

"I'm comatose."

"What?"

"Comatose. I can't help them. I can barely talk." A breeze ruffled the water on the pool, blurred the reflection of rocks and bushes like an Impressionist painting.

"You're talking right now, aren't you?"

"They'd be better off."

"Wait a minute." Roxanne leaned toward me from her chair, her face uncomfortably close to mine. "That is com-PLETE-ly ridiculous. Didn't you ever study about those rhesus monkeys in school?"

I shook my head no.

"Rhesus monkeys. Proven studies that showed baby rhesus monkeys do better than orphaned ones, even if the mother only lets the baby lay on her chest. Nothing more. Touch only."

"Rox, don't make up stories just to—"

"I'm not bullshitting you. Look at any decent child psych book."

"So you're saying if all I can do is let my children sleep on me, they're better off?"

"Exactly."

"Some mother. What if someone else could mother better, do more?"

"It's not the same."

"Really?" My voice bloated with skepticism.

"Really." She snapped the book open with a force that nearly ripped the pages.

That night I walked into Ken's study and told him about my backup plan, my Julie-for-Miriam broken-bride-swap-out to form the Jewish Brady Bunch. Ken sat at his desk and listened for several minutes.

Being a good salesperson, I listed all the benefits of the transaction. He'd have a wife who was Jewish, who could organize things, hold her own in social situations. She'd get a husband, a father for her son. Our children would have a mother who could handle the social pressures of Dallas. She'd dress Becka, nurture Andrew, and advise them both on the balance between academics, sports, and play. I hadn't talked to Miriam about the plan but was sure she'd see the strengths. Me, well, I'd disappear. Ken let me ramble on to the point I thought I'd convinced him.

Ken sighed, put his forehead in his hands. "There's only one problem." He looked up. "I love you. I can't help myself. Although you're trying pretty damn hard to convince me otherwise." He moved his hands prayer-like in front of his lips. "I don't want anyone else."

"But why? I'm wrong for you, wrong for the kids."

He pulled the album I made for his birthday from the shelf, flipped to a photo of the four of us. "You're saying this is wrong?" He pointed to the photo. "What's wrong with this?"

I lay down on his couch, crunched in a ball, and closed my eyes.

"You're sick, Julie. You're just sick, that's all."

"How can you still think that?" I whispered.

"It's all I can think."

"What if this is me? From here out?"

"This isn't you. We meet with that new psychiatrist, Ackerman, next week. We're going to review options. You're going to get better, you'll see." He closed the photo book. "Hey, did you ever get the handle on your car door fixed?"

"No."

Ken wanted me to replace my car, a forest green Explorer. He hated the ketchup stains on the ceiling and the sour, lingering odor of old chocolate milk. I agreed the Explorer needed to be replaced, had even test driven a few SUVs, but my Explorer felt so familiar, so comfortable. The driver's seat had worn to the contour of my butt. I knew the controls. A new car? I couldn't take one more ounce of change. Before we left for spring break, the handle on the driver's door broke. I rolled down the window and reached through to let myself out. This problem had persisted for over six weeks.

"Let me fix the handle for you," Ken offered. "Let me fix something I can fix."

I felt relieved, helpless, stupid that I'd let the problem fester for so long, yet happy he'd make the repair for me. "Thank you." I got up from the couch, walked to him sitting at his desk, and hugged him. I kissed him on the top of his head. "Thanks for putting up with me."

The next day Ken returned home early in the afternoon, before I'd picked up the kids from school. The garage door opened and two cheerful beeps sounded to let me know he arrived. Ken found me in the living room, pondering an article in *People* magazine.

"Come see." He danced. "Come see your car."

"My door handle?"

"Yes, they did a great job."

Why was Ken so worked up over a door handle? I pulled myself from the couch and walked with him toward the garage. He flung the door open and flipped on the light.

A new maroon Escalade engulfed the space once occupied by my Explorer. The car looked swollen, gorged, an SUV pumped on steroids and muscles flexed. Ken opened the car door to expose the SUV's flawless, tan leather interior.

"Do you like it? Do you like it?"

Without a word, I strode into the house. I pushed open the door to the backyard. Ken followed.

I stood with my back to him, facing the pool. I watched the water tumble over the rocks.

Ken grabbed my shoulder, turned me to face him. "What is wrong with you?" He shook me, then let go as if he'd burnt himself. "You test drove this car. You said you liked it."

I took a step backward, dangerously close to the pool's edge. "You are trying—" each word gasped for air, "to replace me."

"What? No! That Explorer was a piece of shit! It smelled!" He turned away from me, toward the house.

I whispered to his back. "It was—"

He turned back; hands open, pleading with me. "My God, there were ants under the back seat! Did you know that—where all the crackers dropped."

I crossed my arms. "It was my car."

"Your car. Right. The car looked like yours, a relic of the Polish Autoworkers Union. Give it up, Julie!" He turned, disgusted, and started to walk back to the house.

"It was my car."

"Take the car back." He stepped back toward me. "Suit yourself. Look as blue collar as you are." Ken held the key out on his palm and then flipped his hand. The key dropped on the limestone path inches from my feet. The key's silver edge glistened against the pale backdrop. Ken marched back into the house, slammed the door with a force that shook the panes of glass.

Blue collar?

I was stunned. "Blue collar" as an economic epithet, like "cracker" or "white trash." Never had I linked my father's history to shame. They were legends, my father's family, people who became doctors and engineers and earned doctorates—when fifteen family members once shared the same bathroom. Now, in this new light, they became blue collar, because my grandfather worked on an assembly line, because my father's family helped fix other people's plumbing. All the accomplishments, all the books read, everything reduced in the intonation of two words: "blue collar."

Part of me wanted to throw the key in his face. *Damn right! That's my history; these are my roots.* My history was part of me but not all of me. With two words, he shunned the texture that made me who I was.

I envisioned the key in my hand, ready for flight, a red splatter on his forehead. I wanted him to bleed. But he was inside, long gone. The key sat on the ground, the moment past. Good thing I didn't throw the key. A fit of violence would have satisfied him, proved his point. Emotion over intellect, obviously inferior.

The sun beat on my head, made my hair crisp. In Virginia, even on the hottest days the sun never felt this hot. Sticky, yes.

Uncomfortable, yes, but the sun never sucked all the moisture from the air so my scalp cracked.

I missed Virginia, the dogwoods. Dallas lacks the right soil for the trees of my childhood. Not enough acid. Too much sun. Insufficient water. I knew the risks of survival when I planted my dogwoods but planted anyway. The one that died withered, burnt. The tree never took root.

I missed my family. I missed my mother's honesty, the way she cut things open and lay them bare. When she cut, she hurt, but I knew what was real. I missed the way my father held me. I missed my brothers and sister.

My family, as it was, no longer existed. My father was dead. My siblings were cast across states and countries. My mother lived in a town I never considered home. My connection to my history faded, a trail lost in a long hike through the woods. The path back evaporated with each step that led forward to something better. Now in that better, that vague space defined as more, I felt diminished, less to the point of being inconsequential. In my own home, with my own spouse, I was homeless.

I picked up the key. The sunlight reflected off silver. I shoved the key in my pocket.

A week later, I went to Ackerman's office with Artie and Ken. The room felt claustrophobic, tucked away, designed so people could enter and exit without being noticed.

The three men laid out their ideas while I sat on the couch, huddled in a corner. Ken had searched the Internet, found a place called Sierra Tucson nestled at the foothills of the Santa Catalina Mountains in Arizona. One of Ackerman's other patients went there for alcohol treatment. Artie wondered if I should stay at home, get in a routine, and have friends support me.

Their words floated around me, distant, as though I were a laboratory specimen who hadn't responded to stimuli as expected. I left the couch, curled up on the floor, fetal position. I knew I looked crazy, but I didn't care.

"Julie?" Artie moved over to where I lay on the floor. "Are you okay?"

If I ignored them, pretended I could not hear, perhaps they'd disappear. *They don't exist. They don't exist. They don't exist.*

"Julie! Get up off the floor!" Ken snapped. "Don't you have an opinion on this?"

They don't exist. They don't exist . . . Maybe they'll forget I'm here.

Ken erupted. "Julie!"

"Let her go." Ackerman motioned from behind his desk. "She's not hurting anyone. We must remember that depression is a temporary problem. Most serious depression works through a cycle in six to nine months. More than anything, we need time to pass."

"I can't watch her anymore." Ken got up and stood over me. "She's wearing me down, wearing our friends down. She's going to do something I can't stop."

They don't exist. They don't exist.

Artie knelt next to me, put his hand on my hip. I felt him gently take my arm. He helped me to my feet.

"Julie, come on, get up." Artie guided me back to the couch.

"She's got to be functional," Ackerman warned. "I can't recommend that she go if she's acting this way."

"This is a bad day," Ken said. "Yesterday she swam in the pool, didn't you?"

The pool, underwater, sounds muted. I felt at home there. I nodded.

Ken opened his calendar. "They can take her. I've already called them. All they need is your approval." Ken nodded to Ackerman.

"Sierra Tucson is a month commitment." Ackerman tapped his pen on the desk.

"I'll miss Becka's birthday . . . ," I mumbled from the couch. All three men turned toward me.

Ken walked over next to me, rubbed my hand. "If you don't go, you might miss her birthday anyway. Miss all of them." He kissed my forehead. "I'll handle the party. She won't miss a beat."

"Time," Ackerman repeated. "All you need is time. Things will change."

To what, I wondered. To what? From my perspective, my life seemed a cliff-like drop from January to May, with no relief. I wanted the ground. I wanted the ground even if the impact would shatter me. I wanted an end, by their hand or mine.

"I'll go," I said.

21

Sierra Tucson

*T*hree women tittered on the couch beside me. All comfortably round, past fifty, connected with sparks.

"Really!"

"And then what?"

"I don't believe it."

"How *painful.*"

They spoke with wisdom of each other's interior terrain although their conversation revealed they'd just met. The women hurled themselves into their stories with such fury no one noticed my eavesdropping. I picked out their names—Doreen, Mary, and Sandra. Their afflictions followed like surnames—Alcoholic, Drug Addict, and Compulsive Shopper. They cackled and howled, tossing one outrageous moment after another into the cauldron of their stories, each one stirring the broth.

Doreen carried her extra twenty pounds with confidence, as though she intended them to be there. "Then—" Doreen's thick brown hair bounced on her shoulders. "I bought ten outfits and poured myself a tumbler of Grey Goose."

"That landed you here?" Mary's e's dragged and revealed her southern roots. Her practical clothes and dated glasses suggested motherhood as a main profession.

I shifted in the chair. My thighs stuck to leather.

"One small other problem," Doreen's bubbling flattened. "I wrapped my car around a light pole."

"Ooohhhh," Sandra, dressed in all black, clicked her tongue. "*That* would do it." She crossed her long legs.

All three were silent for about ten seconds. Then their mouths twitched. A torrent of giggles filled the room. They howled. Tears trickled down Doreen's round cheeks.

Mary mentioned her struggle with Ativan. I felt my throat tighten. My psychiatrist had prescribed Ativan, but I hadn't yet taken my first pill. I feared the drug's addictive potential. Ativan soothes the patient, allows the panic stricken to climb out from underneath the covers. Mary's addiction started with a legitimate prescription. Her panic attacks kept her from dinner parties so essential to her husband's ascension up the corporate ladder. Ativan made social interaction, every interaction, easy. Soon Mary convinced several doctors to prescribe Ativan. She waltzed through every event in her day.

"D-d-did you say Ativan?" I stuttered. All three women turned and noticed me for the first time. "Sorry, I d-d-didn't mean to listen . . ."

"Oh, hon." Mary bounced over to my chair. "We're all friends here." She touched my shoulder. "So what's wrong with you?"

Before I could answer, two male guards dumped a tall, unshaven man with wire glasses in the chair next to me. I jumped.

"Don't worry," one of the guards said, "Jonathan's harmless. Heroin addiction. He might take a day before he wakes up." On Jonathan's right arm, a swirling dragon tattoo reached from his wrist to his armpit. He sprawled in the chair, limp, arms flopped upward and legs spread wide.

"Poor dear," Doreen and Mary said in unison. Doreen squatted next to Jonathan, caressing his hand. Mary positioned herself between his sprawled legs with her hands planted on her knees. She whispered words of comfort as if Jonathan could hear her. Sandra moved to the far side of the couch and rolled her eyes to enlist my disgust at this misplaced altruism.

For the first time in months, I wanted to laugh. Headlines flashed in my brain—"Suburban Housewives Comfort Heroin Addict. Miracles Happen at Sierra Tucson."

Mary turned back to me as if Jonathan's appearance were as normal as a yard boy appearing while we sipped iced tea on her back lawn. "You didn't answer. What's your problem?"

I sank back into my chair. "Depression."

"Depression?" Her brow furrowed. "I thought they only dealt with addictions here. What do they do for depression? Do they give you drugs? Can they cure depression in a month?"

I shrugged my shoulders. I had no idea.

Everyone arriving at Sierra Tucson spends a few days in the Medical Assessment and Stabilization (MAS) area. Once the patient stabilizes, the staff assigns the patient to one of the two dorms on campus. My roommate in MAS curled in bed with her back toward me. Covers over her head and the lights off, she struggled through alcohol withdrawal. Within a day she emerged from her cocoon; by the next day she moved without pain.

I envied her progress. A good cluster of hours for me meant sleep, a sense of hunger, the ability to make minor conversation, and just a couple of suicidal thoughts. Bad hours and bad days followed sleepless nights, filled with uncontrollable panic. I hid in my bed, feigned sleep, but they forced me out. Two days passed and the MAS staff assigned me a dorm and my new roommate.

Janice and I met at dusk. We walked outside, sat on a comfortable bench in a courtyard. The sun began to set behind her, casting a red glow about her head.

Janice suffered from depression triggered by her husband's return to drugs. Prim, about fifty-five years old and conservatively dressed, Janice looked as if she taught English in Topeka. She did. I imagined Janice gently but firmly instructing her students never to end a sentence with a preposition.

Did she really go home to find her husband shooting up? Her husband fell back into drug abuse after a twenty-year hiatus. Janice helped him kick the addiction the first time, but this time his betrayal wounded her.

Janice adjusted her glasses. "I knew if I continued without help, I'd kill myself."

I nodded. Janice's shared experience reassured me far more than any expert. Her words floated like a life raft. She offered no foolproof means for recovery, she made no promises, but for the first time in months someone touched me.

The spark of human contact assured me I wasn't alone.

Despite Sierra Tucson's country club atmosphere, the staff kept a tight schedule. Everyone wore a nametag. First names and the first initial of the last name displayed on sturdy plastic—Julie H., George P., Doreen M. Required at all sessions and meals, the nametag assisted the forgetful or disoriented. The tag also served as a sash of progress, blank at first, but plastered with stickers when the patient accomplished a milestone in recovery or survived another week.

Mary's initial guess about the clientele proved accurate. Most guests had an addiction. The depressed-only guests were easy to pick out. We walked more slowly. We worried about lack of sleep. Bipolar people on a manic swing don't check into treatment centers.

The counselors told us that all addiction has roots in depression. I had my doubts. Doreen, Mary, and Sandra magnetically connected despite their cravings, perhaps because of them. Even Jonathan, the heroin addict, could quote poetry in one breath and deliver a sarcastic witticism in the next. Their lives moved, collided, and crashed. Depression patients' lives stood still, fragile, apart, and encased in a glass cage. I found myself longing for an addiction.

I had more therapy in a month at Sierra Tucson than most people have in a lifetime. Once released from MAS, the staff assigned Mitch Sampson as my counselor. Mitch's wavy hair hit below the nape of his neck but not quite to his shoulder, a trimmed-up hippie throwback. His hair was too long for business but too short for someone who might live in a van.

In our first meeting, the sun blazed through a wall-sized window behind Mitch. Squinting, I focused on his darkened outline as he spoke. "Is it okay if we talk in the open? My office doesn't have windows."

"Sure." I squinted.

Mitch moved his chair forward. "Can you tell me how you got here?"

My words came out slowly at first, like pebbles tossed in a well to test depth. Mitch didn't say much. He didn't jot quick notes to summarize my neuroses. "Hmm . . . uh-huh . . . ," he repeated over and over again.

I blathered. Stories about Ken, my children, my family, my religion or lack thereof, and choices I'd made in my life tumbled out. I defined myself as a spiritual person but not religious. Mitch uh-huhed every point. I began to wonder if he'd fallen asleep, each uh-huh a counselor-perfected snore.

Mitch straightened himself. "So."

I looked for a clock to tell me I'd overextended my time.

"Do you still pray?"

"Well . . . yes." I remembered the electricity that surged through my palms when I meditated—God in high voltage. Lately, my depression yanked the plug.

"How do you pray?"

"What do you mean?" I didn't want to talk about religion, didn't want him asking the *If you believe in God, how could you ever kill yourself?* question.

"Do you say an Our Father . . . make something up . . . what do you ask for?"

My mother had the Prayer of St. Francis on her bed stand throughout my childhood,

Lord, make me an instrument of your peace.

Where there is hatred, let me sow love;

Where there is injury, pardon;

Where there is doubt, faith . . .

My prayer became a one-line abbreviation of St. Francis's. I gave Mitch the line without explanation. "Lord, make me your instrument."

"That's what you pray?" Mitch rubbed his chin. "Interesting. From St. Francis, right?"

I nodded.

He thought for a moment, studied the panels in the ceiling. The silence didn't bother him. "Do you think God is answering your prayer?"

"What?" I rubbed my temple with the fingers of my right hand. His logic made no sense to me. This guy inhaled one time too many. "What are you talking about?"

"Maybe God's answering." Mitch leaned forward. "You're being his instrument by being depressed."

"Are you serious?" I folded my arms across my chest. "I can't do anything when I'm depressed—how could I be God's instrument? I can barely get out of bed."

"I see." He smiled. "Only highly qualified personnel get to be instruments of God."

"No." I leaned back on the couch, arms unfolded. "No, anyone can."

"Oh, anyone, huh—what about a really old person?"

"Well," I huffed, "of course . . ."

"Or a cripple? If you can't even walk, what can you do for God? I guess you think those people are worthless? Or a—"

"No! No, of course not! Nobody is worthless!" My voiced strained. I liked Mitch better when I thought he was asleep.

"Oh, I see," he mocked the sudden revelation, "everybody but you. You go by the Julie Gold Standard."

"Mitch," I snapped, "you're missing the point."

"Are you sure? Sure I'm missing it?"

"Yes I'm sure. I can't help anyone in this state."

He nodded with a twisted smile on his lips. "You can't understand God's role for you, so the situation must not be God's intention."

"That's not what I think . . ." I looked at my watch. *Aren't we out of time? How long is he going to keep me here?*

"Julie, have you ever thought that being an instrument might mean letting someone else help you?"

"What?" My voice scratched with anger.

"Maybe you have something to learn by being helped. Maybe someone else needs to learn by giving to you—ever thought of that?"

I crossed my arms sharply and slammed into the back of the chair. The soft leathery cushions defused the impact, like an angry child trying to stomp her feet in a foot of snow. Mitch knew he'd provoked me but ignored my reaction.

I left Mitch's office with his words scrambling in my head. He turned the prayer upside down. In receiving, we give. *Could that be right?* My Shabbat friends had told me as much. They had time, energy, and desire to help me, even if I never returned the favor. *In receiving, we give.* That idea conflicted with lessons learned and enforced my entire life.

By the end of the first week, I'd assembled an odd conglomeration of depressed friends. My depressed friends' shared experiences acted as Cliffs Notes, bringing us close. My roommate, Janice, and I bonded immediately. She woke me every morning and made me read the dated passage from our *Gentle Reminders* affirmation book. She pulled me out of bed and pushed me forward. Janice knew how to progress when her whole self ached with indifference. She dragged me with her. She made me eat breakfast.

George T., a retired textile kingpin from North Carolina, ferreted out my shrinking guise each day in the cafeteria line. Without reason, he adopted me. Maybe George had a habit of harboring stray and injured animals, or was raised in the school of helping others. In any case, I benefited. His demeanor comforted me, steady, consistent, a sincere interest void of invasive intrusion. George never thought about taking his life, but he doubted his purpose. He never doubted mine. "Look at your children." His brown eyes were firm under soft gray brows. "You can't give up."

Marcello M. was the fourth and final member of our depressed group, by far the happiest depressed person I'd ever met. Dark, thick curls encircled his tanned face, and his eyes twinkled with his wide smile. He'd convinced me to run with him around the campus. His deep Colombian accent sounded musical. "Jooolie, come on. You said you used to run five miles a day. Try one with me."

I tried and gave up after half a mile, panting and weak. Marcello stopped, chuckled in baritone tones, and pointed out the stripes on a lizard's back. Marcello had a vitality earned from years of questioning his own worth. I felt transparent next to him.

The four of us—Janice, George, Marcello, and I—met frequently in line for breakfast. We asked the critical questions: "Did you sleep? Did the drugs kick in?" Of the four of us, my mood swung most radically, due to my panic attacks. Despite the drugs prescribed and daily therapy, I'd go from bad to worse without a clear pattern.

The head psychiatrist diagnosed me as Unipolar with High Anxiety. Unipolar means always depressed as opposed to Bipolar, which allows for some manic relief from a depressed state. *A depressed depressive, depressed all the time—Unipolar.* The label affixed with a thud. My psychiatrist at Sierra Tucson prescribed a new antidepressant and another medication for anxiety, but these drugs only dulled my senses, making me morbid and blurry instead of just morbid.

The days moved slowly at Sierra Tucson. Between required meals, individual therapy, and primary group therapy, we'd squeeze in other forms of rehabilitation. Speakers promoted the twelve-step program and surrendering to a Higher Power. I wrote grief letters for my Dad's early death, my innocence stolen by a twisted military doctor, and my lost self.

One counselor asked me to draw a picture of myself when I was truly happy. I drew myself as a child, alone, walking in the snow. When my marker outlined my stick-figure childhood body, I felt a wave of well-being, comfort, contentment, a state I'd forgotten. I lingered in the room, afraid that once I left, the feeling would vanish. My class members streamed out, and a new group entered. Late for my next class, I placed the drawing in my folder. I stepped out of the room and shoved that sense of wholeness back into an obscure file in my gray matter.

Each day went like this: classes, twelve steps reviewed and revisited, group therapy, personal therapy, private talks, private walks, and meals. Contact with family was limited, e-mails printed and faxes delivered, phone calls only allowed at specified times. By the second week, Marcello invited me to a sunset prayer service he and a few others, mostly men, did every evening.

Handwritten and copied several times over, the service derives from a Native American tradition. As the sun ebbed over the mountain, we formed a circle, faced west. We thanked Father Sky and Mother Earth for the rain, the rivers and oceans, for our place in the world, a small part of something much greater. When we finished our prayer to the west, we concluded with *Ah-Ho all my relations.* We then turned north and prayed for protection. *Ah-Ho all my relations.* We turned east and asked for rebirth. *Ah-Ho all my relations.* We turned south and requested the power to heal ourselves. *Ah-Ho all my relations.*

Finally we looked to our own shadow, that part of ourselves that we hide from others, that we reject as ours. We asked for the courage to reveal our shadow and love our whole selves. *That under my shadow lies much of my gold. Ah-Ho all my relations.*

The words felt mysterious, yet fundamental—foreign, yet mine.

I returned to my room in a meditative state. My mail waited for me, a fax from my mother or an e-mail from Ken, the typed words exact on the page. I read them, knowing that their words flowed from the east, from Dallas, from Virginia. *Ah-Ho,* I did not feel reborn.

They loved me, I loved them, yet I felt distant, detached. I imagined their faces when they finally understood what I knew as truth. My shadow was me, all of me. Everything else stemmed from the mirage I once created—the mirage they still chose to believe.

In primary group therapy, we spent most of our time in preparation for Family Week, where each of us would have a confrontation with critical members of our family. As my Family Week approached, Mitch thought I should have a dress rehearsal to help me prepare for the session with Ken. I eyed the vacant chair across from me. The members of my group encircled me and whispered words of support.

"Okay, Julie, talk to the chair." Mitch tapped the back of the empty chair. "Tell Ken what you feel."

"Ken, you really hurt me when you said—"

"No, come on, Julie." Mitch rose to his feet. "You've got to separate the person from the action. Say 'Ken, when you said this, I felt . . .' You choose to feel something; no one can *make* you feel."

Semantics always ignite a small fire in my brain. This whole *when you did, I felt* phraseology irked me. Even in my Unipolar state my jaw locked.

"Fine." I cleared my throat. "Ken, when you replaced my Explorer with the Escalade, I felt angry." I remembered when he dropped the key on the limestone path, the sound of "blue collar" as the words baked in the sun.

A couple of men in the group exchanged glances as though I'd lost my Unipolar mind. Quinlan R., unable to contain himself, blurted out, "So what's the problem?"

"He didn't ask me." I blinked my eyes to regain focus.

"For God's sake, woman!" Quinlan's British accent made my objection seem all the more ridiculous. "The poor man was trying to surprise you!"

"He wanted to change me." I stared at my feet, the straps of my Tevas. I knew my explanation sounded crazy, but that's the way I felt. I couldn't translate the feeling into the right words. "Upgrade me."

"What?" Quinlan's muscles tensed in his neck. A body builder, the rightward kink to Quinlan's nose suggested he'd often used his fists to make a point, and he lost more than once.

"The Explorer was too blue collar . . . I needed to match—"

"What the hell?" Quinlan's black brows surged together on his forehead. His voice reached a pitch not heard from him in three weeks of therapy.

"The house."

Quinlan snorted his disgust, crossed his arms, and slouched back in his chair.

"Quinlan, I don't fit in my life. I embarrass my husband and children. I'm like a puzzle piece ground into the wrong space."

"So you're going to kill yourself? Take back the damn car."

"It's more than that," I mumbled. My problem was much more, but how do you shrink ten years of compromises into a few sentences? My life didn't feel like mine. "My brain is stuck. I look at homeless people. I'm like them. I'm sure without the money I'd be panhandling on a street corner. I can't think any more . . . I want my life to be over." I stared at him with dry eyes.

The tears had stopped months earlier. My depression numbed me. I could see everything but touch nothing, feel nothing.

Quinlan sighed, "That's pathetic."

"You're right," I agreed.

Mitch hesitated, trying to determine if this were a breakthrough moment.

"God, Julie," Quinlan grunted. "If you felt like this, why didn't you shoot up?"

My mom arrived first for Family Week. I dreaded the encounter with her. What excuse could I give to my mother for a suicide attempt? What when you do's could be so terrible for me to justify my pulling a knife on myself? Mom already felt guilty as hell; the exercise seemed redundant.

When I faced her, she had tears in her eyes, but she cracked some joke in a feeble attempt to make us both feel better.

My session with Ken followed. We faced each other. I started first. "When you took my Explorer and bought the Escalade, I felt like you were trying to erase me, change me into something you wanted."

He looked down. When our eyes met again, he mouthed, "I wanted you." I felt distracted. I thought of why I married him. I loved the way he touched me. He made me laugh. I loved the way his mind worked. He wanted me with a passion no one else ever did.

Ken articulated his defense. "When I found you with a knife in your hand, I felt betrayed." Point, counterpoint. "When I left you at Zale Lipshy, I felt frightened." Ten points for Ken. "When I think of our children without a mother, it makes me sad." Done. How could I possibly justify my actions?

Ken identifies flaws and finds solutions with disturbing alacrity. My depression stood as the first obstacle he could not overcome. Usually Ken looks at a problem and discovers an answer instantly. His clarity is often humiliating. I love to watch the wheels turn in his brain and see his solution emerge light-years before anyone else's. I hate when he solves my problems, figures out my life before I can. *When you always know the answer before me, I feel stupid, less than I am.* Why wasn't I brave enough to say that?

Ken misses things, and those things are my strengths. The problem is I can't pinpoint my attributes. I feel them in my gut, they whisper in my ear. I'm not even sure if my strengths are mine or just channeled energy. My best traits don't fit in a résumé.

Quinlan pumped Ken's right hand while he patted Ken on the shoulder.

"Take care of her, man." Quinlan gave Ken a firm man-to-man look. In this short chair-to-chair encounter, Ken won everyone's affection.

That last week at Sierra Tucson, I forced myself to act well. I claimed the antidepressant took hold and my panic attacks subsided. All my energy focused on feigning wellness, in a place with no daily pressures and a therapist around every corner. I knew I could not hold the strings of my existence this tightly on the outside—but I wanted out.

I threw stones in a pit in a star-lit ceremony with the rest of the graduates. They named their stones Jack Daniels, Klonopin, Spending Frenzy, Heroin, and Cocaine. I had a hard time naming mine but finally decided on three: Fear, Panic, and Hopelessness. The stones sparked on contact as we threw them into the pile.

After the ceremony, I walked back in the darkness by myself. A full moon lit the path, throwing shadows from the boulders and cacti. I noticed Doreen, Mary, and Sandra sitting outside around a wrought iron table, more somber than usual. We'd all be leaving the next day. Despite promises of contact, everyone knew we'd never be closer than at this moment.

The next morning, I said my good-byes as I scurried from one person to the next and asked each one to sign my *Gentle Reminders* book. All of us did this, signing our names and writing our contact information. We acted like high school seniors, trying to capture a prophetic one-line thought in our best friend's yearbook.

Janice and I packed our bags together and embraced a long time before we left our room. She pulled away from me and put her hands on my shoulders.

"One step at a time."

I needed some time to think before Ken arrived. I wandered on a dirt path that led up a small hill, away from the buildings. From that spot, I could see the mountains in the distance, craggy and stark. In the wide span of desert before me, the wind blew sand into a tunnel, which spun and dispersed before gaining momentum. The breeze brushed against my face.

Someone emerged by my side. "Jooolie," Marcello whispered. "Beautiful, isn't it?"

I nodded.

Marcello turned toward the west, toward the mountains, took a deep breath, and exhaled.

Ah-Ho all my relations.

"Come—" He put his arm around my waist and guided me toward the path. "Ken is here. Time to go home."

22

Threads of Connection

You put on skates, go around once, and sing 'Happy Birthday.'" Ken ushered me into the car. "How hard could it be?" Ken planned Andrew's birthday party at the Thunderbird Roller Rink, two days after I got back to Dallas.

The roller rink was dark and noisy. My ears filled with the murmur of parents' conversations, the clunk of rollerblades hitting the floor, and the slam of a pinball machine. A waft of fresh popcorn stole the last bit of breathable air. I couldn't see anything. Panic rose in my chest. My eyes adjusted from the midafternoon sun outside.

Becka clutched my hand and pulled me toward the bench. I laced Becka's skates, then my own, head down, more busy than the task required. I didn't want to see anyone. I didn't want to explain my month's disappearance.

Andrew rounded the edge of the rink with his friends; his ankles tipped inward on rollerblades. His eyes darted my direction once. Andrew had been distant since I got back.

Becka saw me and insisted I be the same person she had always known. At five, she needed help and asked. "Help me tie my shoes." "Feed me." "Get me a glass of water, please." She didn't notice how I teetered on those skates. She held my hand—me, the girl who skated every sidewalk in the neighborhood and loved the bumps as a kid. I gripped her small hand in mine, struggling to balance.

We left for Santa Fe immediately after the party. I moved from a suicide attempt, to a locked ward, to a rehabilitation center, to a place with no counselors or psychiatric supervision and no friends for support. Many of the Shabbat women objected but couldn't deter Ken from his plan.

When we reached Santa Fe, I climbed to the roof. I hoped the sky might once again provide some salvation by scenery. The Sangre de Cristo Mountains filled the northern view, the city of Santa Fe and the Sandia range in the southeast, and the Jemez Mountains in the west. From my lips, the prayer I learned at Sierra Tucson emerged, "Ah-Ho all my relations." I waited. I felt nothing. I waited longer. Nothing.

Cut off from my community, my family, my husband, my children, and God, I felt numb. Depression blunts nerves, divides the holy trinity of body, mind, and spirit into three separate and lesser parts. Without depression, I know things to be true even when they are intangible. With depression, I split. My mind and body conspired against each other while my spirit, my rudder, splintered.

My first week in Santa Fe, I awarded myself my own degree in psychiatry and weaned myself off one medication and cut the other one in half. My plan lacked any scientific justification. I didn't consult my psychiatrist because I feared he would refuse to cooperate.

I vowed to think only positive thoughts. With a gratitude journal in hand, I listed five things every day for which I was grateful. *Hell, it worked for Oprah.* I thanked God and offered myself, free of charge, as his servant.

Three days later, I climbed to the top of a mountain and planned to toss myself over the edge.

For the first time in my life, details were important. I got a babysitter. I made a date with Ken and some friends that night so Ken wouldn't suspect anything. I wrote in my journal that I looked forward to taking a long hike a few days later, on Thursday, by myself. This was a lie. By Thursday, I figured, I'd be dead.

I hoped my children might find this journal note and somehow prove my suicidal fall an accident. Maria, a sitter I'd hired through a local agency, watched my two children. Although I'd only met Maria that afternoon, I figured she'd be a kind soul who could comfort my children when they found my body. I got in my car, pulled out of the drive, and headed toward the ski basin.

Raven's Ridge seemed a good place to die, a trail with a cliff overlooking Santa Fe Baldy, another peak about five miles to the northeast. Four years prior, I'd hiked Raven's Ridge, tailing a determined Andrew who wanted to touch the snow in June. Becka called "bird" to the gray jays that followed us, perched in her baby backpack that peeked above my shoulders. On that hike, with two kids under three years of age, I craved freedom. Looking out from that cliff, my children in tow, I felt free, for a moment. The view gave respite from diapers, play dates, and tedious parent-child commands.

In June of my suicidal summer, I returned to Raven's Ridge in search of a different sort of freedom. The trail started much as I remembered—pines, wildflowers, and switchbacks. My thighs ached. Finally, the cliff appeared.

I had imagined my suicide jump as a swan dive. For a brief moment, I'd be suspended in air, wind through my fingertips, defying gravity, like my Dad in top form on the high dive at the public pool. Dad always took three steps, lifted his right knee, jumped, and then glided with his arms outstretched. He flew through the air, then hit the water with a tidy splash.

My dive would end differently, gravity forcing me downward, the granite pulverizing my skull and crushing my bones on impact. When I glanced down from the cliff, I knew the fall wouldn't work. I might get stuck in a tree or on a ledge, fall twenty feet, snap my spinal cord, and paralyze myself. What a mess.

Disgusted, I scanned the horizon. Santa Fe Baldy's dark green peak wore a thin stole of white clouds. The scenery made me stop. Tiny drops trickled from the edge of my baseball cap, down the back of my neck. I shivered. Rain dripped off the pine needles, raced by my boots, off the cliff to the stream below. The cap kept my face dry.

The debate began in my head. *Are you sure about this?*

By this point, I'd stopped answering those questions.

Okay, let's say under the best possibility there is no afterlife. Let's assume you just die. Do you want to lie in that ground and feel nothing, see nothing? Miss this? Forever?

I gazed at Santa Fe Baldy and felt she stared back at me. Clouds swirled, drops of rain fell harder. I'd never climbed that mountain. I wondered what I'd see from there. "Go back," Baldy seemed to whisper. "You're mistaken. It's not your time."

Stepping back from the cliff, I turned and bolted down the hill. Water flew and mud splattered. The damp leaves slid and released a musty odor of upturned earth when my feet hit the ground. Already late for dinner, I worried Ken might suspect something. I pushed a branch out of my way, pulled my cap down, and ran harder. *He'll send me away again.* The thought of another stint in a mental ward spurred my pace.

I jumped in the car and raced down the slick road. The wheels slipped on the sharp turns. When I opened the car door in the garage, a water bottle tumbled out with me. Maria gaped when I ran past. I ripped off my clothes, jumped in the shower, sped to the restaurant—thirty minutes late. I'm never late. Breathless, I told Ken and the other couple, between apologies, that I took a wrong turn on the trail and got lost. They nodded and bought my lies without question. Then I heard a voice just like mine recommending the ahi tuna appetizer.

Just like that. As if nothing happened.

I told Ken about my mountain hike a few days after I stared over the ledge. He looked beaten. My lies confused him, hurt him, and left him in a state of constant alert. He could no longer determine if what looked like progress was progress.

After the hike to the mountain, I decided I would no longer lie in my journal. The entries show my desperation.

God, I don't know if you are there . . . Please guide me and help me see the lessons in all of this. Right now I just feel tired and battle on an hourly basis with an overwhelming desire to kill myself.

Mom and my sister Eileen got bits of how I felt but never the whole story. I didn't want to poison them. My depression felt like a contagious cancer or mental leprosy. I saw the energy drain from others as they spoke to me, wanting to help yet not knowing how. My friends and family wanted me to live, at least at the beginning of that summer. By August, they didn't want me to die, but their impatience showed. Even the most devoted family members and friends shielded their eyes. The suicide red-alert light flashed daily, hourly, by the second. They were tired.

Depression wears even the deepest love to a fine thread. The visits, the talks, and the phone calls must've seemed pointless as I replied with the same blank answers. My friends and family didn't understand, but they helped. Interference helped. Those threads, however worn, distracted me. They bought me time.

To carry out a suicide requires solitude, a final disconnection. I couldn't kill myself when the phone rang with a call from Mom or Eileen or Miriam or Kate or Tara, or when I read a card from my brother Patrick, or when my brother Teddy sent me his personal, worn copy of Thich Nhat Hanh's *Peace Is Every Step*. Teddy wrote me a message on the front flap: "To my sister who taught me the joy of poetry. May each day be a poem."

I found Hanh's concept of "The dandelion has my smile" difficult to absorb when eyeing knives, cliffs, ropes, or Clorox for my demise, but I knew Teddy loved that book. He gave me his only copy. His one small act made me pause.

The threads made me realize the impact of my death on people I love.

No, I can't kill myself today because my sister Eileen is coming to Santa Fe in two weeks, and she's never been to Santa Fe. My sister is an artist, and I knew she'd love Santa Fe as much as I did. I didn't want my death to taint her impression of the city. That thought stopped me, not the idea that Eileen might be traumatized by my death.

When Eileen's sixteen-year-old son Cameron came to visit for a week, I thought, *No, I can't kill myself while Cameron is here.* That might scar Cameron for life, and Eileen would be pissed.

My friend Kristi visited us our last week in Santa Fe. I thought more clearly with her. *I can't do this to Kristi.* She and I have a friendship that extends over twenty years. She inspires me. I suspect, until that summer when I tried to take my life, Kristi viewed me as her rock. Our friendship was a strong thread.

On the shelf in my office, I keep a painted rock Kristi gave me that summer. Kristi visited us every summer in Santa Fe, and every summer she introduced a new art project in which the kids and I participated. That suicidal summer, we painted rocks.

Kristi picked a brown flat stone to paint for me. On one side, she painted a spiral with the words *Julie—every cloud . . .* On the other side, I noticed a thin glittering line of silver around a cloud. Without words, Kristi let me complete the thought—*has a silver lining.*

My cloud, that inescapable cloud, blocked my vision for nearly a year. I'd jumped from Dallas to Tucson to Santa Fe, and my depression followed, undeterred. When I returned to Dallas that August, my depression waited for the right moment to take action. No one could protect me from myself twenty-four hours a day forever. When we left Santa Fe that summer, we piled our gear on the top of the Escalade, protected with tarp and secured with a rope.

I did not find my miracle cure.

When we left Santa Fe, I didn't look back as I usually did and watch the mountains shrink until they flattened into desert.

I couldn't. I didn't think I'd ever return.

23

In Retrospect

*B*y the time we reached the Texas border, Ken had arranged Mom's flight to Dallas. "I've done all I can," he whispered over the phone. "I can't take it anymore."

I didn't want Mom to come. Since Mom never accepted the concept of leaving something unsaid, this visit would not be conciliatory. I feared she'd peer at me through her glasses—the ones that magnify those deep blue eyes of hers—and sum me up.

Three days later when Ken went to work, as Mom slept in the guest bedroom and my children in their beds, I drove my burgundy Escalade into the garage. With the garage door closed, I let my SUV run.

Even now, I can't believe I looked my mother in the eye when I planned to kill myself the next day. I did. Secretly, I hoped she'd see something wrong and set me straight. God knows she'd read my mind before. Sometimes she only needed to hear "Hello" over the phone. She usually asked the right questions, suggested answers, and then expounded on the repercussions of my actions like any good psychologist.

But not that summer.

That summer, I asked the question, not her. I asked the question every morning. *Is my life worth living?* The question screamed in my brain, but Mom assumed I knew the answer to that one.

Yes. Yes, life is worth living.

She couldn't fathom another answer, but I could. Mom looked past me, through me—unable to recognize me. This frightened, stuttering person I'd become couldn't be her child. The child she knew had spunk, gumption—she set her own rules. How could a person who lived life without bounds see death as her only alternative?

I didn't think about the repercussions of suicide. One small death drops in a pond, and the ripples push everyone to a new place. I've learned so much about those ripples since I tried and failed to commit suicide.

A friend of mine, a gorgeous, artistic woman—one of those who always looks hip and stylish but doesn't fight her age—told me through tears that her father had killed himself when she was three years old. Three years old. She didn't even know him. Yet thirty-five years later, his death still twists the corners of her mouth.

She fears the suicide seed. Will she be tempted? Will she see warning signs? I tried to comfort her, reassure her, while my own guilt raged inside me. This could've been my daughter, haunted by my one fatal mistake for more than three decades.

That August morning, I didn't think about the ripples. I was a rock who wanted the comfort of the bottom of the pond. *Let me fall quietly. Let the fall stop. Let me rest.*

When the garage didn't work, when a fluke of architecture saved me, I told them. I told Margaret, Mom, Ken, all of them. I'm not sure why. Maybe I figured I'd never reach the bottom of the pond. Maybe part of me didn't buy the whole rock analogy anyway. Maybe I realized that at the bottom of the pond, there is only mud, thick mud that suffocates. The pain survives in a new form.

After my morning in the garage, the process for my recovery started. Dr. Galen suggested ECT, and nearly a month later, I underwent the first treatment. The weeks prior to ECT are blurry, a common side effect. One memory, however, remains vivid: our annual summer party.

In retrospect, throwing that party seems an act of desperation: Ken's stubbornness to keep his life in order. Was he wrong, or was this positive thinking?

Every August, for eleven years at that point, we threw a summer party. This party expanded over the years from a few adults in swimsuits to a full-fledged carnival with a dunking booth, massage therapists, snow cone machine, and a magician to entertain the kids. We expected 250 attendees. I enjoyed the beginning and end of the party typically, but the middle overwhelmed me. Too many people, too many cursory conversations—this type of party wasn't my style.

Ken loves big parties, as do my children. The larger the event, the more outrageous the attractions, the better. I participated each year because I find joy in their joy. So once a year, I forced myself to be a comfortable host despite my discomfort. The delight in Ken's eyes, Andrew's swagger, and Becka's smile far outweighed my unease. Besides, the party was only one day—the party usually lasted eleven hours, but for only one day out of the year.

The August of my suicidal summer, eleven hours seemed like an eternity. I dreaded the questions, the stares, and the whispers about my mental state. As the day approached, I felt my apprehension building. I coached myself in the spirit of the Little Blue Engine that Could: *I think I can. I think I can.* I didn't want my family to be disappointed.

Ken filled the oversized coolers with a different sense of determination that year—a job with a beginning, middle, and end—something he could accomplish. The vendors rolled in the dunk tank. Andrew and Becka skipped and sprinted, circling the tank as it filled. Eddie Deen's set up the barbeque: chicken, ribs, corn on the cob, fluffy white rolls that most years I dipped deep into the sauce.

Bin after bin of food unloaded, the thick smell inescapable. I turned away, repulsed. *Too much food. Why do we need all this?* Ken unloaded the last bag of ice. He smiled and waved. I squinted, waved back, and walked inside the house.

The party started at 11:00 a.m. At 10:30 a.m., the phone rang.

"Julie, it's Rox, are you out of your mind?"

"What?"

"You're having the party, in your state, are you crazy?"

"Well—"

"Fucking unbelievable."

We were silent, long enough for Roxanne to ask me if I was still there. I tried to explain, but Roxanne didn't buy my reasons. Roxanne was angry with Ken for insisting on the party, furious at me for not protecting myself. She begged me to come to her house or some other place where I could seek emotional shelter. I refused.

A half-hour after Roxanne called, guests filtered into our backyard. I stood near the house, so I could duck inside if the conversation got too uncomfortable. Another family flowed into our backyard, then another, then more. Soon the rumble of conversations drowned out the music.

Andrew and Becka convinced Ken he should be the first victim in the dunk tank. Ken climbed onto the wooden bench that rested above the water. A teenage boy hurled the ball with adolescent fury but no direction. The ball whizzed past the target.

Ken taunted the boy and the next girl in line. "Come on! Is that all you got?"

The girl lined up, threw, and caught the edge of the target, but the seat held.

"Almost, almost," Ken laughed, "but not quite. Any of you strong enough to knock me in?" Drawn to the scene, I stepped down from my office patio, onto the grass. Becka jumped up and down in line, ready to toss the winning shot.

I felt a hand on my bare shoulder. Shelly, the wife of one of Ken's employees. Bubbly, blonde, and somewhat round, Shelly's white straw sunhat dipped over her right eye.

"Julie! So good to see you. Wow. You've lost a lot of weight! How'd you do it? Atkins? You know, I tried Atkins once and lost twenty pounds, but piled it right back on. What's your secret, you've got to tell me."

"Uh . . ." I felt flat, a life-sized cardboard version of myself. Across the lawn, I saw Becka walk three feet from the target and hurl the ball with all her might. Ken's head disappeared into the tank. He emerged, soaked.

"Oh, come on. Just between us girls." She hunched her shoulders up in anticipation of my instant weight-loss secret.

"I'm not really trying . . . ."

Kids fought in line for the chance to dunk Mr. Hersh.

"Oh, that's right!" Shelly slapped my arm, already guessing the answer to the question she asked. "You're one of those crazy runners, probably training for a marathon. That's it, isn't it? I bet that's what you did."

I nodded, and she talked on. I bobbed my head, blended in, and smiled at her one-sided conversation. *The less said the better.* Be boring. Be mediocre. "Mediocrity is the best camouflage . . ." I read that once, in *The Power of One.*

"Well." Shelly sighed, took off her hat, and wiped her brow. "I don't give a damn what my thighs look like. I'm gettin' in that pool."

The party had grown from a few families to over a hundred people in less than a half-hour. Half-naked bodies of all shapes and sizes spewed into our yard. People hovered at tables, ribs at their lips, the burnt red smear of sauce on cheeks, fingers, and discarded napkins. Bees zoomed over half-empty soda cans.

I watched the families from the sidelines, hesitant to get too close. Bare arms and legs gave way to more bare arms and legs and sweat. Ken stood in the middle of the crowd, waving his arms, deep in the throes of some story he'd created. At the punch line, they all laughed and begged him to continue.

Roxanne appeared at my side. Her eyes filled with tears when she looked at me and shooed her children to follow their father. "Some party, eh? Couldn't pull yourself away?"

I felt thin, paper thin, almost invisible. I turned toward the house.

"Do you want me to come with you?" she asked.

I shook my head no. "Just tell Ken something. Tell him I went for a massage."

"Are you safe?"

"Yes, I promise. I just need to be alone."

But there was no alone. The massage therapists were stationed in our bedroom, in the exercise room, and I could hear kids upstairs. My office was a thoroughfare.

I locked myself in the powder room next to my office. I looked at my watch. *3:00 p.m. Seven more hours to go.* I hid for fifteen minutes, until someone knocked. "Just a second," I said. "Let me finish." When I exited, a young boy squirted past me, still wet from the pool. He slammed the door.

Ousted, I stood in my office. The crowd swarmed in the yard, visible from every angle through the ten-foot windows that lined the east and north walls of my office. I wanted to feel outside when I was in, I told the architect. I got my wish, but my life's design left me nowhere to hide, nowhere that felt safe.

That August felt and feels surreal, even years later. A suicide attempt, then a long wait for ECT, interrupted by a party with massage therapists, a dunk tank, and hundreds of people who either didn't know or pretended they didn't know.

When September came, events in the world became as frightening as the inside of my head. On the morning of September 11, I went to play tennis with a friend. The news of the first plane hit when I sat at a red light. I turned the radio off, unable to listen to bad news.

During the first game on the tennis court, my friend's husband called and told her about the second tower. We raced to her house. When we turned on the news, the Pentagon had been hit. My thoughts moved in slow motion. *My brother, my brother Matt works in the Pentagon. I better get home and call Mom.* After several calls, I finally reached Mom. Matt was alive. I never doubted that he survived the collision. I don't know why, but I knew he wasn't dead.

Matt told me he stood in an office with his commanding officer one ring from where the plane hit. He pulled bodies from the wreckage, commandeered a golf cart to do everything he could to stop the screams. He couldn't reach them. The flames were too intense for him or others to enter without protective gear. The bombproof glass installed at the Pentagon after the Oklahoma City bombing turned the Pentagon into an impenetrable furnace.

Matt received a medal for his efforts, but he doesn't consider anything he did heroic. My brother saw bodies charred, lives slaughtered in a type of warfare that left veteran military personnel in shock. "There was no honor in this," Matt said months later when I asked him to show his medal to my children. "We were unprepared."

A few days after September 11, I checked into the psychiatric ward at Zale Lipshy. My comfortable life led me to a locked ward, while Matt's horrific experience tested him but left him intact.

This seems odd. Shouldn't Matt's horrific experience lead to insanity more than what happened to me? What did happen to me? Life, death, wealth, a loss of direction, prolonged bad weather?

In instances like these, I have to remind myself that depression is a disease, a disorder, a disproportionate reaction to the situation at hand. Circumstances might aggravate mental illness, but not every mind reacts in the same way. From any perspective, my life situation seemed placid, certainly nothing that might cause a person to commit suicide. But I did try to kill myself. The urge to commit suicide is not logical and can't be explained or cured by things that might seem the right ingredients for a perfect life. Depression is a matter of life, electricity, and chemistry that we have yet to understand.

Luckily, I found my piece of lightning that saved my life. That blast allowed me to think differently. Ken said I called him a few hours after my initial ECT session. I don't remember the call, one of the memories lost in the weeks surrounding ECT. Ken remembers. He tells me my voice sounded like the woman he knew as me.

"Come pick me up," I told him. "I'm cured."

24

Santa Fe Baldy

A year changes everything, doesn't it?" I stood with Kristi at the turn for Raven's Ridge. We wanted to climb Santa Fe Baldy, a hike of about fourteen miles.

Kristi nodded. Kristi, like my father, makes her best points in silence.

A year earlier, I'd made that turn to Raven's Ridge with a plan for a swan-dive suicide. The hike to Santa Fe Baldy doesn't include Raven's Ridge.

We continued through the gate to the Pecos Wilderness. The aspens tapped their applause for each breath of wind. We lost the need to speak.

Kristi sighed. We'd been lost in our own thoughts.

"Remember what you were like? Remember that argument?"

"Which one?"

"I asked, 'Do you think I'm stupid?' You told me, 'No,' Then I argued, 'If you're so mentally addled, do you think I would spend this much time with you? Ask your advice?'"

I tried to remember the conversation but couldn't. Another moment lost to ECT. "How'd I respond to that?"

"You told me that I pitied you." Kristi looked shaken—part angry, part hurt.

I glanced down the left side of the trail, a steep drop. My eyes stung. I tried to blink them back, but the tears came. "I'm sorry I did that to you. Sorry you had to experience this."

Kristi hugged me, an awkward hug, arms around the pack, maneuvered past the tube and nozzle of my CamelBak. I hugged her tightly, then wiped the tears from my face.

"You're alive," she said. "That's what counts."

We continued down the trail, and reached a meadow, a wide-open field to our right. Wildflowers dotted the grass. "I'm so glad," I said, "that depression is behind me. That we can share hikes again."

"Me too," Kristi nodded. "Me too." Kristi reached into her pack and pulled out the map. She smoothed the map on a flat rock. "Looks like we're about halfway."

I glanced at my watch. "Halfway? Are you serious? Let me see that thing." I pulled the map from her hands and followed the trail. She was right. I'd underestimated the trip by three hours.

Our cell phones were useless at that distance. There was no way to contact anyone to tell them we'd be late. Kristi offered to turn back, but I insisted we push forward.

"We won't get this chance again for years," I said as I folded the map. "The kids will be fine. Someone will call Ken. He can pick up the kids."

"Won't they be upset?"

"I want this, Kristi. I do everything for them." I handed the map back to her. "Just this once. They'll live."

Kristi shook her head, moved the dirt with her boot.

"I need this." I clenched my fists with dramatic flair.

"Okay," she laughed. "Let's go."

We spent another hour winding upward. The afternoon skies filled with dark clouds.

About a mile from the summit, we saw our first strike of lightning in the distance, about ten miles away. I glanced over my shoulder south, the direction from where the lightning came, to see Raven's Ridge staring back at me.

"We've got to turn back," Kristi urged. "Lightning moves fast. We're above the tree line."

The peak was a mile away, but I took another step toward the summit.

"Julie! We're sitting targets."

I felt the waft of cool air from the storm hit my face. Kristi was right. She knew the signs; the ascent wasn't worth the risk, but I stepped forward.

"Julie!"

I tried to explain the inexplicable. I had to reach that point. I knew my need to reach the peak was stupid, but I also knew the storm was far away, with the wind blowing away from us. To continue was risky but moderately risky, not crazy. Besides I had small children. I'd followed the rules like a robot over the past year. Therapy, eat well, sleep well, more therapy, don't push too hard. Watch yourself. I needed to breathe.

"I have to make the top. This is more than a mountain to me."

"That mountain will be here tomorrow!"

"But I won't. I leave tomorrow for Dallas. I won't be back for a year."

"I will come back with you! I promise!"

I smiled. "It's okay, Kristi. I'll be okay."

"Fine—" she turned on her heel. "I'm going back down." She headed south as I strode north to the summit.

From the top ledge, I could see for miles. The desert spread to my left and the wide green of Pecos to my right. Drops hit my face as one step followed the other. I walked with Raven's Ridge to my back.

I reached the summit that day—the black storm sheet in the distance, moving farther away, as I had predicted. Lightning flashed, splintered, filling that portion of the sky with terror. From my perch on top of Santa Fe Baldy, I watched in awe.

The rain subsided. I raised my arms to the sky and felt the wind against my back.

25

Relapse

I wanted my story to end on the mountaintop. My depression conquered, I bound my words with a black spiral cord and sent my story to fifty of my friends. In that first version, I had depression licked.

With the help of therapy and medication, I'd gone without a serious dip back into depression for four years. I felt healed.

After many changes in my life to reduce stress, I determined I no longer needed medication. I consulted Dr. Galen, my psychiatrist, whom I still saw on a yearly basis. I sat in Galen's office and laid out my plan.

"What do you think?" I went for the close. "Can I go off medication?"

Dr. Galen twisted in his seat, agitated. "No, NO. Given the severity of your depression, I can't in good conscience approve that."

"Why?"

"Statistically you are high-risk. As your doctor, I have to tell you—rejecting medication is a bad idea."

"Fine." I folded my arms in front of my chest. I planned to stop taking the pills. If Galen wouldn't support me, I'd monitor myself.

I'd done the hard work of depression. I removed stress from my life. I set boundaries with my mother-in-law, my community, my children, and my husband. I made peace with my economic status. I hired a personal shopper so I could feel more appropriately dressed for the business and charity events that landed on my calendar. I joined an Episcopal church, attended weekly services, and also celebrated Jewish holidays with my family. My solutions weren't perfect, but what in life is? More important than perfection, I learned to have an opinion, to have a voice.

All these changes and my continued good health convinced me that I should stop medication. "I feel good, therefore I am cured" is a faulty conclusion reached by many who suffer with mental illness. Many go off medication and drift back into crisis. I didn't want to be one of *them*, the ones who needed medication for the rest of their lives.

Books I read, by psychiatrists and spiritual healers, supported my idea. One noted psychiatrist advised that antidepressants could be used like antibiotics, unnecessary once the wound healed. Most spiritual healers I read professed a whole soul didn't need medicine. I considered myself whole, so why take the medicine?

My medication had no noticeable side effects. Why was taking a small purple pill so disconcerting? When I swallowed, the pill reminded me of my weakness—that small, soft spot above the back of my heel that I wanted to forget, my mental illness, my Achilles. The pill reminded me that my depression was only under control, in remission, an idea I didn't want to accept.

The summer I decided to forgo medication contained a series of exciting trips. A safari in Africa, an eighty-mile hike through the Sierras, and a camping trip with Andrew at Yellowstone filled my schedule. That summer appeared to be my kind of break—outdoors, immersed in the forest, stretching my body to new limits.

Before the first trip, I finished my prescription. I didn't refill it. The summer stretched before me. My adventures began unchecked, without approval from my doctor or the knowledge of my family or friends.

In September, I let Ken and Dr. Galen know that I stopped my medication—about three months after I had taken the last pill. Ken applauded me. He wanted my depression cured as much as I did. A life without medication seemed to validate my complete healing.

When I told Dr. Galen, he shook his head. "No matter what I say," he said, "it is clear you are going to do what you want to do. You seem fine. Let's just meet more often, once every three months, and monitor your progress." I kept the appointments for a while, but his schedule and mine were packed with other, more pressing issues. The appointments spread from three to six months, neither of us alarmed.

For almost two years, my life coasted without medication. I worked on my book, volunteered at the kids' schools and at the Dallas Children's Theater. Our lives seemed steady. I reconnected with my family of origin with phone calls and e-mails. Most of my family met in Mexico over Christmas, in a beach house Ken and I had built. We had good-natured discussions about our memories of family life. We argued our own version of what we'd experienced.

When we returned to Dallas in January, the bad weather hit. Day after day of rain and gray weather. The newspaper reported that winter was the wettest since 1928. I felt the grayness. My body began to match the weather.

By March, the leaves on the rose bushes turned an odd yellow color, riddled with black spots. "Too much rain," our landscape man explained. Despite the leaves, the red blooms held, less vital than in previous years, but they appeared deceptively healthy. I only noticed the leaves when I looked closely one morning. We sprayed for black spot, a fungus common for roses. The rain persisted and hampered our efforts.

I cried a lot, set off by the smallest things. After several weeks of my weepy tenor, Ken suggested that I take my antidepressant or at least make an appointment with Dr. Galen. I snapped at Ken, sure my tears emerged from hormones. My depression was behind me, a thing of the past.

The stress piled higher. I bought an apartment in a retirement community for Mom against her wishes. She had agreed two years earlier that the apartment made sense. Mom wanted to live in Harrisonburg, near her friends, far from any of her children. When the apartment became available, she refused to move.

I knew we needed a plan; we had to have a course of action as Mom aged. I knew if we didn't, her care would fall on me, at a time when I couldn't handle the extra responsibility. Mom called me multiple times a week, angry about my decision. "Why are you doing this? I'm so depressed." Mom didn't cry, she accused. "Why are you trying to put me away?"

The conversations drained me, made me realize that despite Mom's years of counseling and daily meditations, her own physical deterioration was something she couldn't face. Like her daughter, Mom had a knack for denial. My New York–born Mom had a Scarlett O'Hara approach to aging. "Tomorrow," she'd say. "I'll think about that tomorrow."

Other bits of stress piled on as the gray weather continued. Becka applied to a host of private schools and was accepted everywhere, so we weighed and debated her choices. My sister hit a midlife snag, so I talked to her multiple times a week on the phone. She helped me when I was depressed, and I wanted to be there for her in the same way.

Ken suggested the idea of moving to London for the next school year. I liked the idea of living abroad, but I'd look out the window and stare at the gray skies. *Could I survive a year of this weather?*

Finally, Andrew's bar mitzvah loomed in October. He got the idea that he wanted to make a movie about World War II veterans as his "mitzvah" project, a required community service project for completion of his bar mitzvah. Ken told me we were crazy when we started the project, and as usual, he was right.

The project exploded into a huge undertaking; Andrew interviewed eighteen local veterans, and I worked as his crew manager. I downloaded all the raw footage and realized we were stuck. Neither of us knew anything about filmmaking. I feared Andrew would fail because of my poor parenting, because of my inability to be realistic and set limits. I sat at the computer, spending hours to make one miniscule change to the film.

The project made me realize the high-tech world had blazed by me without a glance. Either my brain had slowed, or thirteen years out of the industry had left me software learning-impaired. Either option eroded my confidence. The pessimistic voice in my headed chided. *Fantastic ideas or impossible fantasies? What do you think?*

The bar mitzvah represented something deeper too. As I drove Andrew to Hebrew tutoring once a week, I realized Andrew was Jewish.

This seems obvious, but with his bar mitzvah approaching, I felt the pain in a new way. The two of us would never share the same religious history. Andrew would never understand communion or many of my other Catholic traditions.

Andrew also didn't seem to have a strong connection to his spiritual self. The bar mitzvah process focused on memorization and language. I felt his experience lacked a spiritual element. I wondered if I'd failed him, if I'd omitted some vital component to his personal training.

My friends assured me no thirteen-year-old boys are spiritual. Lighten up! But I couldn't lighten up. I failed to see the humor in anything. I was terminally serious.

I slipped, and slipped some more. I withdrew, grew wary of social gatherings, lost weight. I don't keep a scale but previously snug clothing fell off me, bagging in the seat. In April, Ken went out of town for the weekend. I began to crater.

Miriam sensed I was going astray and offered to help. About 9:30 p.m. one Friday night, I called Miriam. She told me she'd be over in a half-hour.

Becka had already gone to sleep and Andrew asked me to read with him. He read *A Wrinkle in Time*. With only ten pages left in the book, I heard Miriam ring the doorbell. I told Andrew to finish and tell me about the book in the morning.

Miriam and I sat a long time on the stone steps outside my front door. I didn't want my children to hear. I cried in Miriam's arms. Messy tears, tears of frustration, of anger about the very idea that depression might show its face again in my life. She held me, like a mother holds a child frightened by a storm.

The next day at a bat mitzvah, my friend Tara cornered me at the luncheon reception.

"What's with you?" Her dark hair fell softly on her shoulders. " 'Fess up. You haven't been sleeping." She paused, gave me a once-over. "You look like a stick."

I glanced into the courtyard, the sun out finally, an escape from rain. "I'm fine."

Tara shook her head. "Right. I don't think so."

"Really." I wished she would leave me alone.

"Not really. It's back, isn't it? The depression. I can tell by your eyes. Have you seen Dr. Galen?"

Why am I always the one who is messed up? Can't they accept me the way I am? "Well . . ."

"Have you at least made an appointment? You're back on meds, right? Please tell me that."

Great. Drug Julie into the person you want her to be. No way. "I can work it out. I don't want the medicine."

"What?" Tara's voice raised in pitch. "Are you nuts? What is wrong with you?"

"I don't think I need medicine."

Tara whispered the next words low, so no one else could hear them, but I could. "Look, you were in a psychiatric ward. You almost killed yourself. You wrote a fricking book about this. How can you not take action?"

"Well, I, I think I can recover myself."

"No." She shook her head. "No, Julie. Your brain is broken. You must get help. You can't see your deterioration, but we can. All of us."

"All of us?"

"You gave us the manual on your symptoms. Weight loss. No sleep. I read the book, remember? We all read the book. What's it going to take? Suicidal thoughts? Another stint in the garage?"

"No." I pushed away from her. "No, that won't happen."

"It won't happen if you get help."

She was right. I knew she was right, but I didn't want to admit that the symptoms had returned.

I did call Dr. Galen, and I started back on my standard medication. Within a few days, I crashed further, suicidal thoughts pounding in my brain.

How did this happen? I called Dr. Galen and scheduled another appointment. I couldn't take nine months of this depression again.

When Ken and I met with him, Dr. Galen suggested ECT. Another round of ECT felt like complete failure. Psychic failure, spiritual failure. *Whole people do not need ECT.* I felt guilty. Guilty that once again, I dragged my friends and family through this morass, this sludge I should be able to prevent.

When I picked up Andrew from school that day, he knew something was wrong. Then twelve years old, he knew what had happened to me during my previous depression. I had told him. Despite his age, I thought he should understand mental illness. Depression ran and runs deep in my family. Although I didn't want to scare him, it seemed irresponsible to not let him know about the chance of genetic transference. We pulled into the main garage and got out of the car.

"Mom," he asked, "is your depression back?"

I looked in those deep blue eyes of his, yellow flecks around the iris. "Yes. I'm sorry. My depression is back."

"That's okay, Mom." He held his palms up, as if he held the answer. "Just go to the doctor, do that shock thing, and take your medicine. What's the big deal?"

What is the big deal? Why couldn't I see my depression like that, as a disease to be addressed?

"You're right. ECT. That's all I have to do." Yet somehow I didn't believe ECT would work again.

He touched my arm. "You'll be okay, Mom."

I smiled. My son turned away from me, not sure what else he should say. I reached out, squeezed his shoulder. "Hey, Andrew, how'd that book end? *A Wrinkle in Time*—"

Andrew shook his head in disgust. "Oh, that book was so stupid. The author couldn't figure out how to end it, so she just made up some dumb ending."

"Really?" I strained to remember. I'd read the book over twenty-five years ago. "How'd the book end?"

"The dad was saved by 'love.' How brain dead is that?"

"Saved by love?"

"Yeah, love, can you believe it?"

I brushed back his thick brown hair. My son looks like me—dark hair and brows, light eyes, and a square jaw. "Andrew." I wondered if a twelve-year-old boy could possibly understand what I wanted to say. "Sometimes the only reason I get through the day is because I love you, and I know you love me."

He squinted, a twelve-year-old smirk. "Huh?" He raised one eyebrow, perplexed, as though he wanted to ask me something, but he didn't. Instead, he turned away from me, shook his head, and walked into the house. As usual, he left the door open.

I stood in the garage and watched him disappear down the hallway into the house. The light shone through the windows, giving the house a warm amber tint. The automatic light in the garage clicked off, heightening the difference.

The thought of the hospital, the locked ward, the fact that my depression had returned made my shoulders ache, the back of my calves feel weary. I leaned against the car. *How did I let this happen again?* I could refuse treatment and try to work through the depression, but I remembered what happened the last time my depression hit. Nine long months, and no real change before ECT. I might get better on my own, but chances were I'd end up in the same spot, eyeing the detached garage with new desperation.

Andrew peeked his head from around the corner. "Mom, what are you doing? Why are you standing there in the dark?"

"I'm coming." I stood and brushed the dust off the back of my jeans where I'd leaned against the car. I hadn't washed the car in ages, too much rain. I walked inside, shut the door, and headed toward my office. I called Dr. Galen's office and scheduled the next round of ECT.

26

I Choose to Live

*T*he clatter of voices, laughter, forks hitting salad plates, glasses clinking in well wishes rose to such a volume that I heard only a rumble, a mass of energy with no clear point of focus. I gulped the last bit of wine. *This will be a tough crowd.*

I'd spoken to larger groups but none so intimidating. We'd just watched a fashion show, pencil-thin women in stunning clothes, who paraded before us as the music pounded. I expected to hate the event, to feel short and inept among throngs of tall, graceful women. Instead, I found myself drawn to the flow of the fabric, the clomp of five-inch heels on the runway, and the power of one model's chocolate brown limbs. The fashion show was theater, good theater. I had to follow this act.

I took my place at the podium. My speech began above the low roar of uninterested, private conversations.

"Life does not always turn out how we plan . . ."

I introduced Jenny, my best friend from high school. Jenny had flown to Dallas for a fundraiser for the Suicide and Crisis Center of North Texas.

The idea of a fashion show to prevent suicide became the fodder of jokes for my invitees. Only in Dallas would these two things be thrown together. Dark jokes zinged on e-mail. Ever commit fashion suicide? Ever kill for that dress?

Jenny and I hadn't seen each other in over ten years, but we still clicked. In my speech, I talked about the gray stone wall at the end of my street. In high school, we'd sit on that wall and dream about our futures. I motioned to Jenny, who sat at my table, surrounded by eight of my close female friends from Dallas.

"Jenny," I grinned in her direction, "correct me if I'm wrong, but I don't recall ever thinking that we'd hop in a limo, in Dallas, Texas, to go to a fashion show, to benefit a suicide and crisis center."

The audience chuckled. I reminisced about how bright our futures looked at that point, how full of possibility. I said the next line slowly, to make sure everyone could hear.

"I would've never guessed that one day I would drive a car into my garage, shut the door, and let the engine run for ninety minutes." I paused. "But I did."

The forks stopped. The voices fell silent. *Oh shit. They really are listening to me.* I met their eyes. "And luckily, for some reason, I am still alive."

My speech continued, propelled by a force far greater than I. I talked about people, some friends, and some complete strangers, who told me the stories of their losses. My brother. My mother. My father. My friend. "It doesn't have to be this way," I urged them. "Mental illness is a disease."

The silence held. My friend who's an actor says actors live for this moment, the pinpoint focus, the hush. I wanted the right words, the right words to help them heal, the right words to broaden their understanding. I felt the weight of my own impossible expectation.

In less than four minutes, I finished and took my seat with my friends. "Great job," Jenny whispered. "Way to make lemons out of lemonade."

I knew she meant the opposite, but the irony struck me. From the outside, my life looked perfect. No one, including me, could believe I almost took my life. I almost did. This strange brain of mine took a world of possibility and created lemons, only to twist life again for a drink tart but sweet.

One bite into my meal, the strangers emerged from the sea of glitterati, the group that paid for a fashion show and won me as the door prize. A woman, in her mid-fifties, told me about her husband, who had killed himself five years before.

"He was so brilliant." She brushed back tears. "Such a life force. Nobody stupid commits suicide."

I smiled, took her comment as an odd compliment. I'd heard the association before. Something about how depressed people are often deep thinkers, that we are more complicated than most. My ego wants to believe this, to think my depression is some trade-off for superior intelligence, but the research proves otherwise. All sorts of people commit suicide—smart, dumb, brown, black, white, rich, poor, young, and old. Mental illness is an equal opportunity disease.

One bite more, and the next person appeared at my side, leaning down to shake my hand as I sat. He had dark hair and wore glasses—his face deep with lines. He seemed kind, gentle. He told me about his daughter. "Eleven of her friends have attempted suicide. And she, too, is suffering from depression."

"Is she here?" I asked. He nodded. "Can I meet her? Take me to her."

He led me through a maze of tables to his daughter, who looked to be about twenty-five years old. I introduced myself and encouraged her to continue to be there for her friends. Six of them had killed themselves. Five of them had survived, like me.

"Don't give up on us." My own words sounded weird. Who appointed me the representative for all those depressed? "We need you."

"You give me hope." She smiled a sad smile. "You make me believe that people can get better." I wanted to hug her, to hold her, and to tell her how much her friends loved her, even if they couldn't live long enough to tell her themselves. Instead, I shook her hand. I offered to help if there was anything I could do. I felt so damn helpless. The father thanked me, and I took my seat.

My friends welcomed me back to the table. Maggie, one of my good friends in the limo group, rubbed my arm, wanted to know where I went. When I told her, we shook our heads in disbelief. That young and eleven suicide attempts. It's a war zone out there, in there, in our own houses, in our own heads. Mental illness is an epidemic, rampant and spreading. *Where is the outrage? 30,000 people a year kill themselves in the US, and we care more about West Nile virus.*

Maggie took a sip of wine and prodded me to try the dessert. "You need to eat something."

We resumed lighter conversation. Jenny talked about London, where she'd lived for fifteen years. She talked about the weather, how the gray drove some people crazy. I'd be going to London for a year in August, and saw the weather as a large obstacle. Still, living in another country seemed the opportunity of a lifetime. If I stayed on medication, watched myself, maybe I could avoid depression. Worst case, I'd come back to Dallas at Christmas. I want to manage my disease, my depression, not be defined by fear of relapse. I felt Maggie bristle next to me.

"Does she not get it?" Maggie seethed in my ear. "Didn't she read your book?"

"She read my book," I assured Maggie, "but she didn't see the connection. The woman hasn't seen me in ten years—go easy on her."

Maggie's blue eyes got wide and she twisted her head. Maggie's a pit bull, born on my mother's birthday. She's kind, but don't make her angry or hurt the people she loves. She counted me as one of them.

I looked around the table. Every one of these women would fight for me, and they weren't even all the people I considered close friends. *How lucky is that?* That night we celebrated, but how different those lives would've been if my plan to take my own life had worked. What would've happened without the ventilation in that detached garage?

Another woman appeared at my side, young, stunning. I asked her if she were one of the models.

"Oh, not me." She blushed, thin fingers to her mouth.

"You could be," I said. "You're amazing."

She told me her story, about her mother who'd battled depression throughout her life. Then the story became more personal, about her own struggle. Her eyes wavered, unable to make contact with me when she told her story. She didn't tell me she tried to commit suicide, but I sensed she omitted that detail. She'd thought about death—from our conversation I knew that, felt the pain in my bones.

"I could never be like you." She looked to the ground, defeated. "I could never be that honest, not with these people. They're all so perfect."

I smiled. I thought of the one woman's six dead friends, of the wife of the man who killed himself. "The perfection is a mask, can you see that? On the inside, some of these people are badly broken. They need all their strength to be here tonight, to put on the clothes, to plaster on a smile so no one might guess the thoughts they had this morning."

She shook her head, rattled. I wanted to tell her something, to give her something that might help her.

"Look." I put my hands on her shoulders. "I know you can be more open about who you are. Let's make a deal. When you are well and able, I want you to speak at an event like this."

"Really?" Her eyes brightened. "You really think I could?"

"Yes. And tell you what—if you invite me, I will come. I will be there for you, like you listened to me tonight."

She smiled, her first smile of the night. She straightened herself and walked off, perfectly balanced on her mammoth heels.

The next day, I scanned the obituaries for the young woman's photograph. I had failed to ask the woman her name, but she seemed the type to have her best photo sitting in an obvious spot in the event she did commit suicide. I flipped through the paper, my breath slow, until I knew she wasn't there.

I didn't see her. I glanced over the dates, the description of deaths, but didn't find a match. Each day for the next week or so, I did the same thing. Ken eyed me curiously over the sports section.

One morning I stopped. By midday I realized I'd forgotten to look. I'd taken my kids to school, run with my friends, and attended a meeting for the next fundraising event for the Dallas Children's Theater. A newspaper sat on the kitchen table when I returned home, but I no longer felt the need to thumb the pages of lost lives. I'd done what I could.

That woman's survival depends on the way she views her world. My words altered her vision for a few minutes, maybe twenty, possibly enough to add up to an hour. Those words can last only as long as her brain allows them to resonate. I helped put the idea there, but she needs to make her recovery her idea if she wants to be well.

In the end, her life is dependent on a fine balance of electricity, chemistry, and choice. Of these three, choice is the most immediate and decisive. Choice pulls the trigger, opens the bottle of pills, or sets the car running in a closed garage. But choice can also put the gun down, put away the bottle of pills, and pick up the phone to call for help.

Aided by a fluke in architecture, I chose to live. My start wasn't glamorous, only a step out of the garage and a truthful admission. With the catalyst of that one small decision, I tried ECT and accepted the help of psychiatrists, psychologists, my Shabbat group, my friends, family, and husband. Will this young woman make the choice to live? Only she can answer that question. I hope she will be as lucky as me. I chose to live.

I choose to live.

Backstory

$\mathcal{E}$lectroconvulsive therapy (ECT) is a psychiatric treatment that involves a burst of electricity through the brain, causing a convulsion that shocks the brain into balance. ECT is often used as a last resort, even though for me and many others, it is the most effective treatment in existence. ECT gained its negative image through inappropriate and overuse in the 1940s and 1950s. The best historical account I've read of ECT is *Shock* by Kitty Dukakis and Larry Tye. If you are considering the procedure, please read their book as well.

Temporary short-term memory loss and permanent memory loss of some events immediately surrounding ECT are two of the procedure's drawbacks. I originally tried to write this book as an autobiographical account but found I couldn't recall the exact details surrounding a few of my feelings and memories. In these situations, I relied on my journals and recollections from family and friends to recount events.

I have changed names, except where friends insisted that I use their real names. I've changed locations and shrunk the deeds of several people into one character when I felt describing all the people would complicate this book beyond any reasonable reader's comprehension. I took some poetic license with color, shoelaces, and minor details.

I have left my own name the same because I feel it is important to treat depression as a disease. I'm not ashamed to admit that I suffer from depression. I did, however, change the names of my family members. Although I believe that the world should have an open and accepting attitude toward depression, the reality is, the world still does not. I choose to be open about my experience, but I don't have a job at stake or have to risk the fact that a future spouse might reject me because of my family's inclination toward depression. My children and siblings are in a far different situation. My husband Ken is content to be Ken.

Although substantially correct, in a few areas I modified events and characters to conceal the identities and make my book easier to understand. As a writer, my goal is to translate life experience into something a reader can grasp or at least question. This is not best accomplished with the mundane details of who said precisely what at a defined time in exact locations. My book is biased by my opinion, even though I've tried to be as objective as possible. Family members have read drafts of this book. Some of them think my account equates with the events of our childhood; others are certain they grew up in a different household. All I can say is that I reached my truth as best as I could.

Acknowledgments

I consider Eden Elieff my literary fertility specialist. After years of talking about writing a book, Eden proved the critical catalyst in its overdue conception. Eden's intensity drove me to that first line where my story could unfold. Kristin van Namen, my editor, no doubt brought to me by some unseen force, was my midwife. Having worked for seven years writing, rewriting, quitting, and back again, Kristin, in a year, coached me to a version that Brown Books accepted for publication. She did this with kindness, humor, and a spiritual insight that helped me craft my story.

Jayme Durant and Janet Harris, editors from Brown Books, helped me refine my book into a size and framework acceptable for the commercial market. Thanks to Jayme, Janet, and Brown Brooks for putting up with my caustic and impatient nature. You have been an instrumental part of that process. Hopefully, this book will inspire people to get help—and may even save a life.

Diane Feffer, my publicist, thank you for your endless avalanche of ideas and unbridled enthusiasm. Your work is superb.

There are various groups of people who have helped write this book: my writing group, my Cooper running buds, my book club, the ASL running group, Kurt Eichenwald, and Pete Earley. Certain individuals went above and beyond the call of duty of friendship. They read multiple drafts, provided meticulous edits, pushed me to continue, and listened to me hash and rehash my story. These are: L.A. Starks, Michelle Williams, Jennifer Fisher, Samara Kline, Rita Juster, Anna Laughlin, Kristi Jamason, Phil Smith, Alison Silberberg, Meg Conine, and Sara Tranchina. You all can see your influence in this book. I love you all and promise not to rewrite Chapter 1 ever again.

Finally, there are those who provided moral support. Tom Johnson, my good friend who I have yet to meet in person, is the inaugural member of the Julie Hersh fan club. Without his strong and steady support, I would have given up on this project years ago. Philip Blackwell, Dave Roy, and Bob Madden, more recent members, have been equally enthusiastic. Others who have helped year after year are: David and Pam Albin, Steve and Chris Reifenberg, Yvonne Crum, Debbye Doorey, Kelly Thompson, Page Victor, the Conines, the Hillsmans, and my Shabbat group. Mom, thank you for your blessing even if you disagree with my depiction of our family life. To my sister and sister-in-law, Paula, thank you for being my long-term, consistent cheerleaders. To my brothers and their wives, thank you for your advice and constant support.

I worry about the impact of this book on my children. My daughter was the first person to call me a writer. My son, a talented writer himself, has always encouraged me to publish, tossing my fears about exposure of our family aside. Kristi dubbed him a "flame licker," fearless. I hope he feels the same way after reading this book. I thank both of them in advance for their courage for any problems they may face because of my honesty about my disease.

And Ken, where would I be without Ken? Not only did he assist me through my depression, but he also relived my depression with every draft of this book he read. My husband has taught me the true meaning of unconditional love. Because of him, I am here, and my words still find their home on blank pages.

Recommended Books

For Understanding ECT:

Shock: The Healing Power of Electroconvulsive Therapy, Kitty Dukakis and Larry Tye

Undercurrents: A Life Beneath the Surface, Martha Manning

For Understanding Mental Illness or Suicidal Tendency:

An Unquiet Mind: A Memoir of Moods and Madness, Kay Redfield Jamison

Night Falls Fast: Understanding Suicide, Kay Redfield Jamison

Darkness Visible: A Memoir of Madness, William Styron

The Noonday Demon: An Atlas of Depression, Andrew Solomon

For Understanding the Process for the Mentally Ill within the US Mental Health and Prison Systems:

Crazy: A Father's Search Through America's Mental Health Madness, Pete Earley

Places to Start for Help:

Mental Health America (National)
1-800-273-TALK

Suicide and Crisis Center of North Texas (Dallas)
214-828-1000